ARIZONA WILDFLOWERS

50 Reference Photos For Nature Artists

By

Al Lodwick

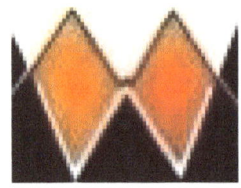
First Edition 2015

ISBN: 9781515351085

DEDICATION

To Ann Lodwick, my wife and best friend for nearly 38 years.

ACKNOWLEDGEMENTS

Scott Mies for encouragement and editorial assistance.

Rachel Lodwick for the Mieswick, LLC logo

Victoria Tubbs for the author's photograph.

INTRODUCTION

This book is designed to give the greatest amount of space to the pictures of flowers, and keep the book reasonably priced. This allows the greatest detail for the artists who want to get everything "just so". For this reason there is no identification of the flowers nor any other facts about the flowers. It was not designed to be a field guide since there are many of these readily available, especially in handier sizes.

If you have special needs or requests please contact the author at allodwick@gmail.com.

The author hopes than non-artists will also enjoy the photographs.

Al Lodwick
Prescott, Arizona
August 2015

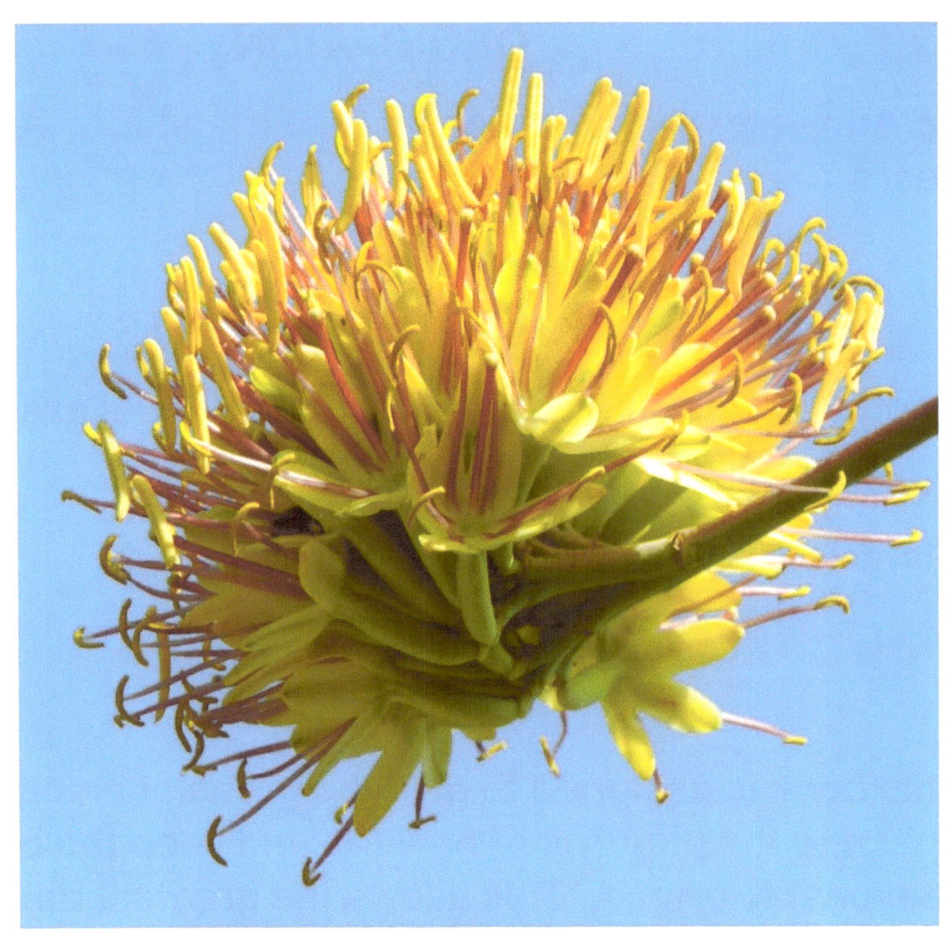

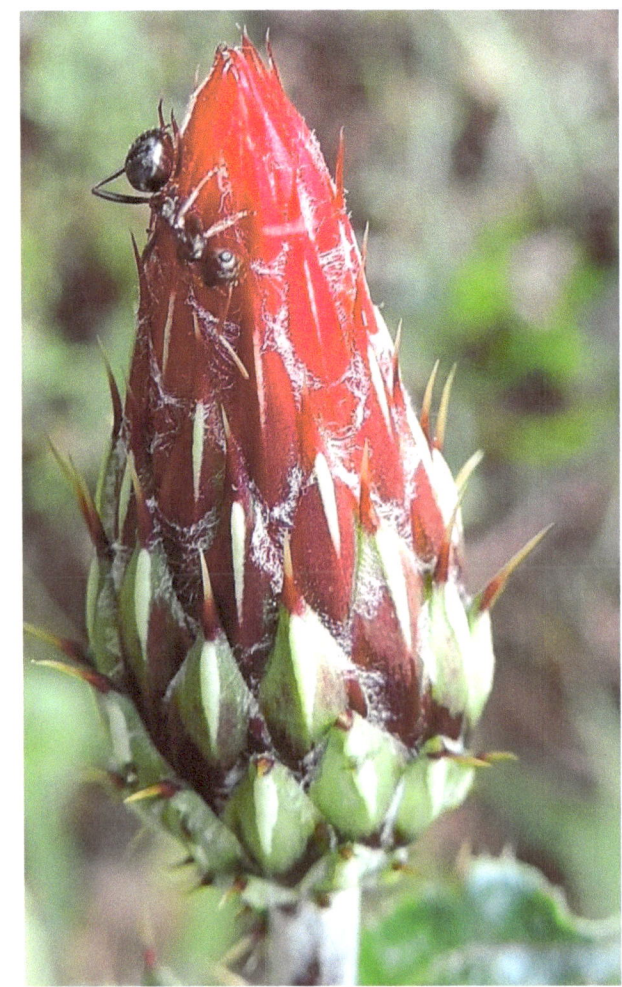

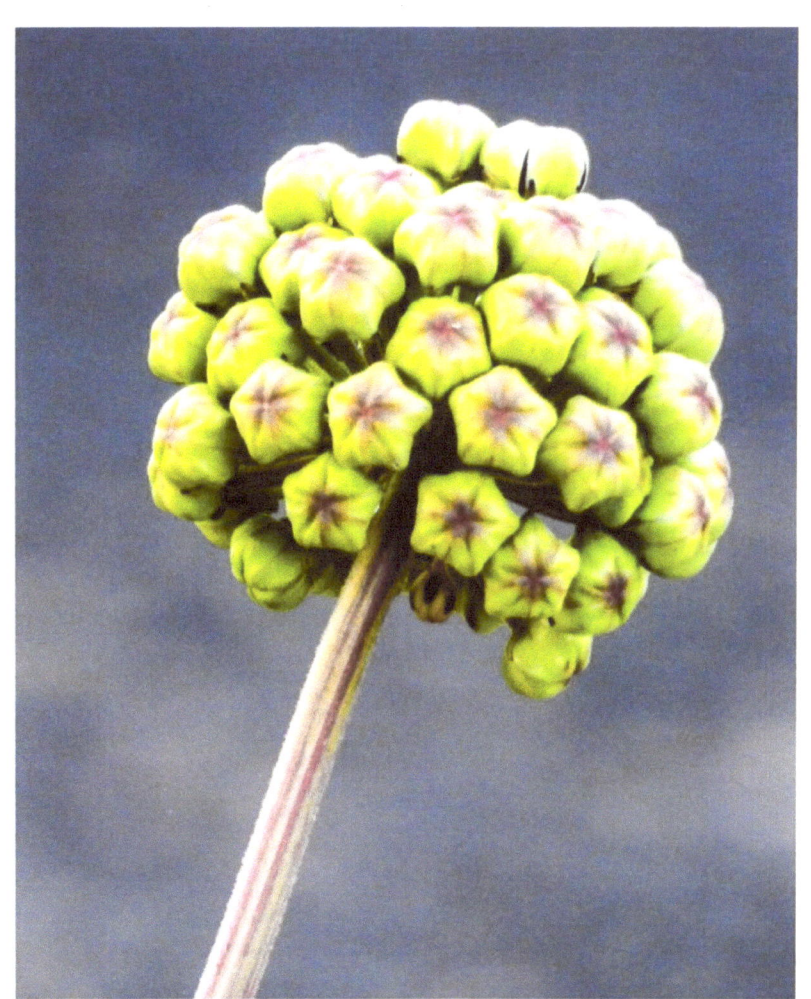

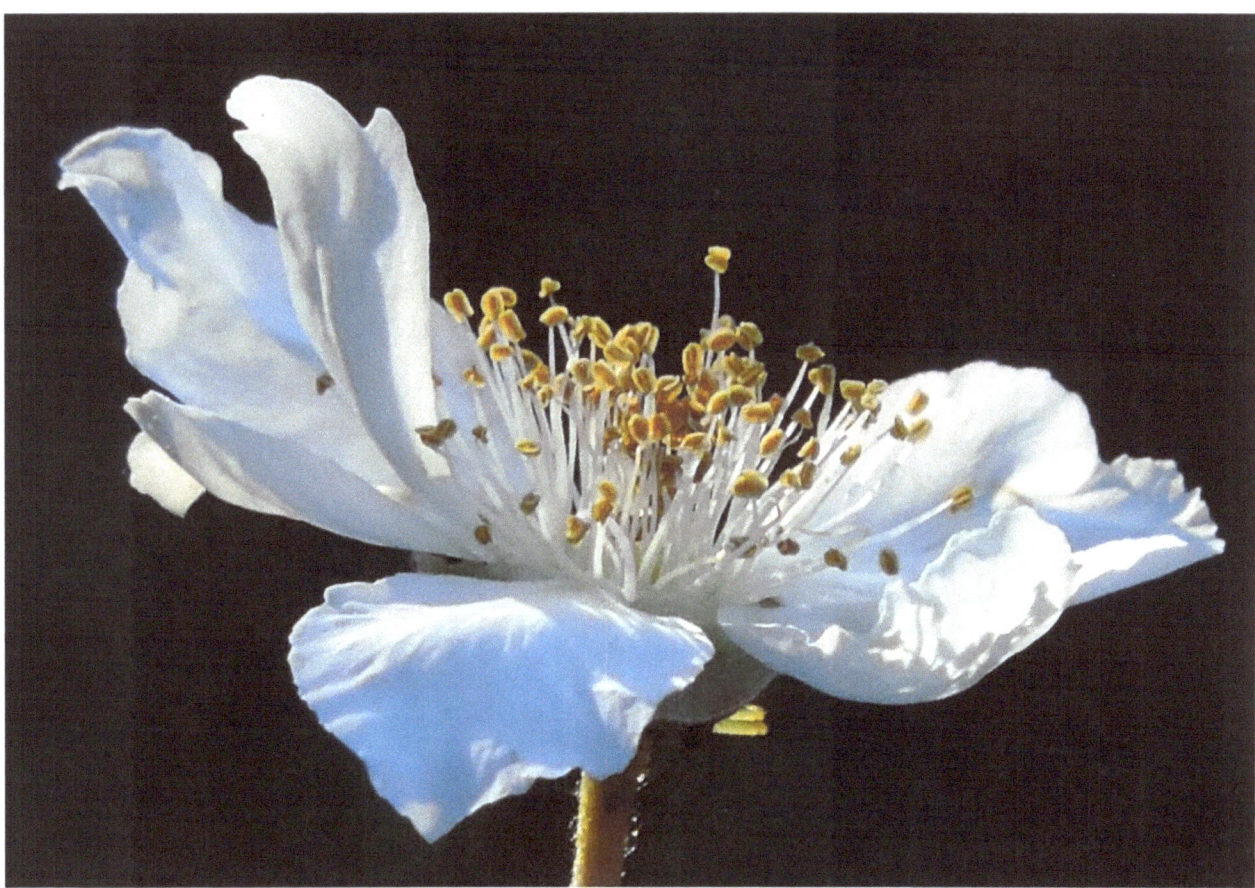

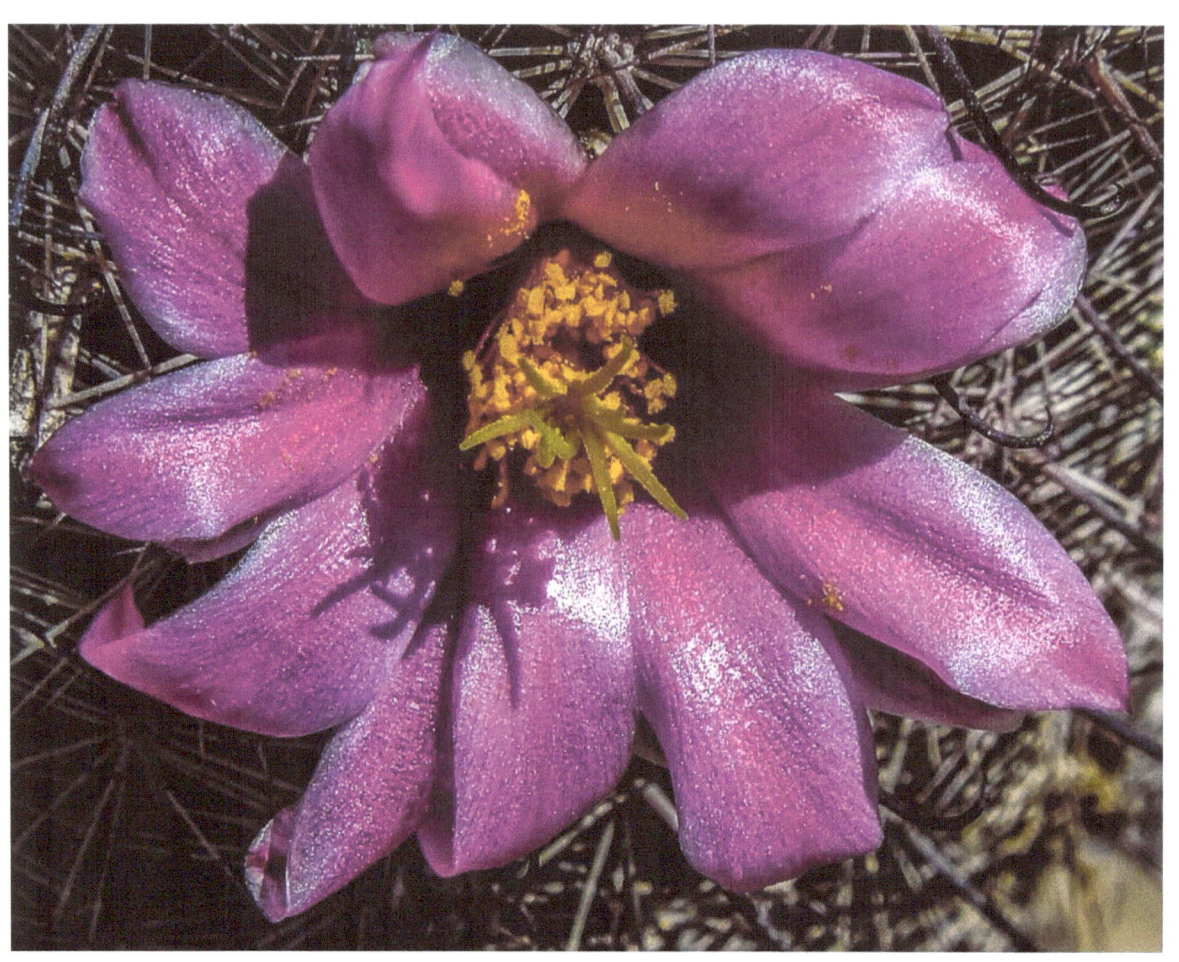

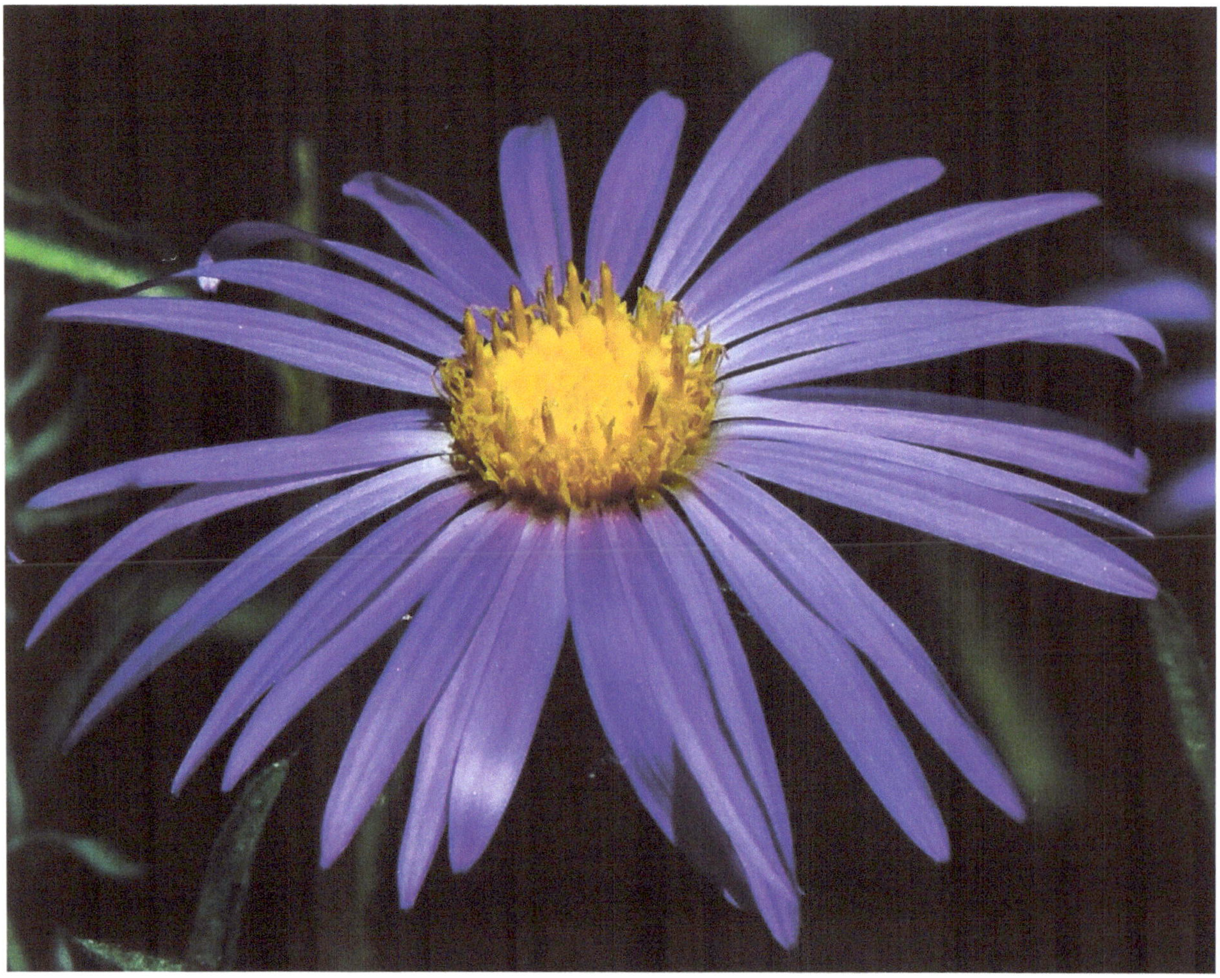

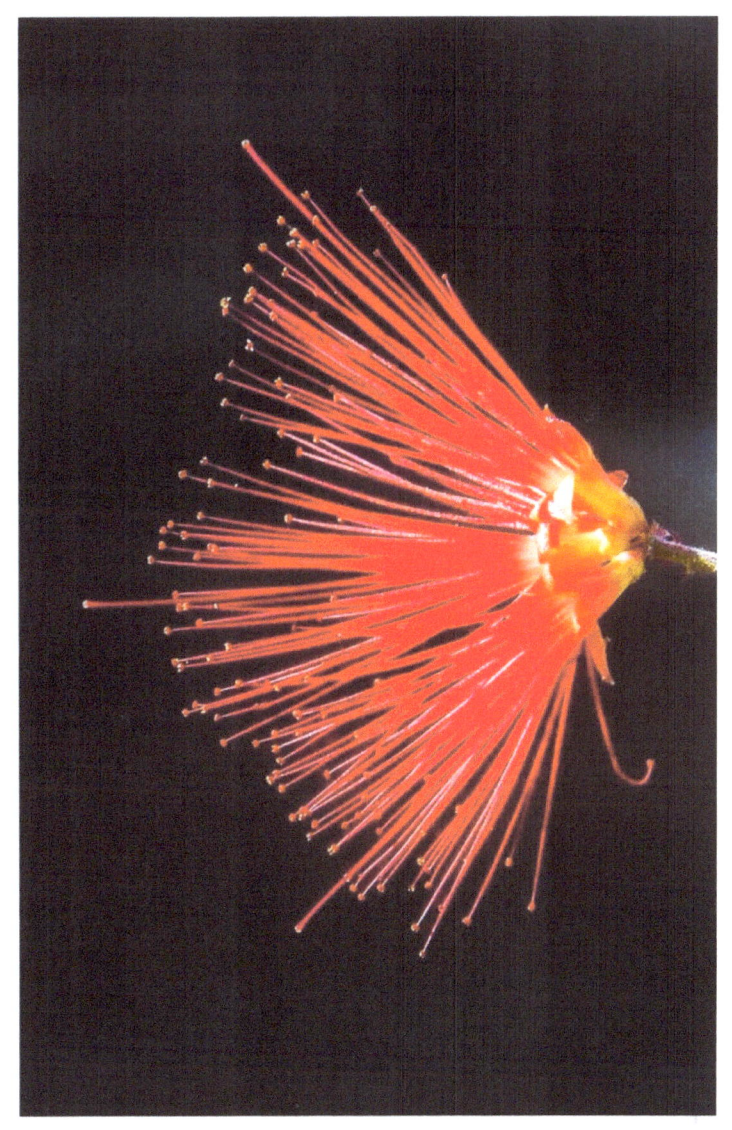

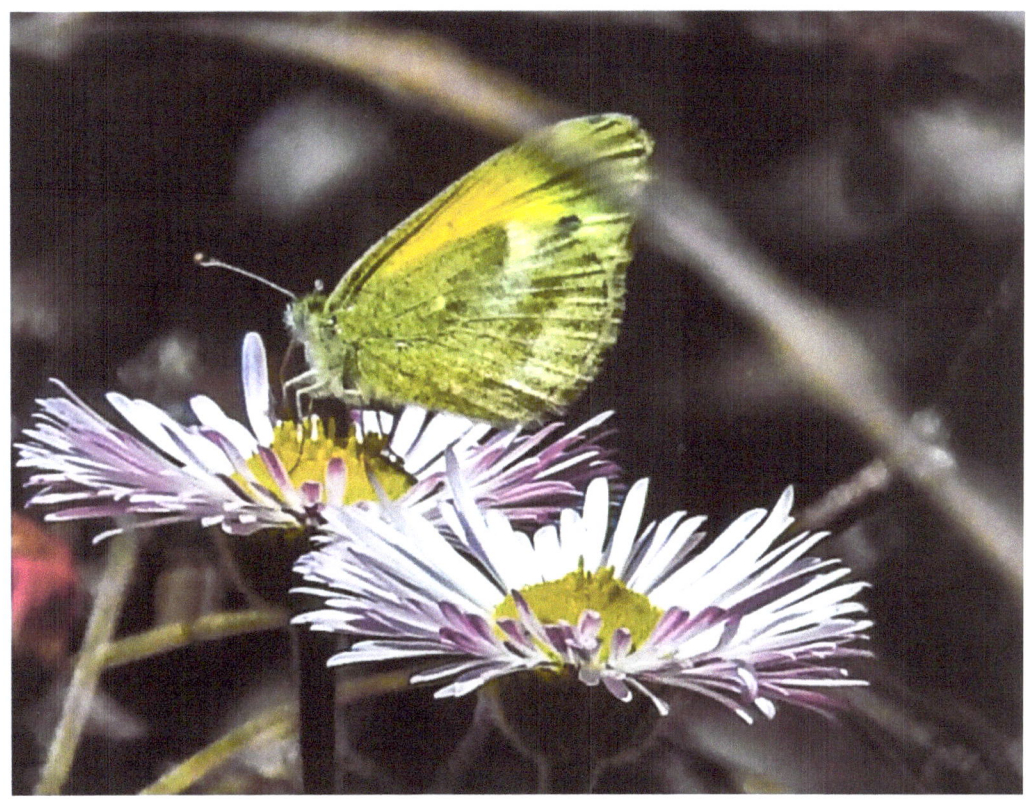

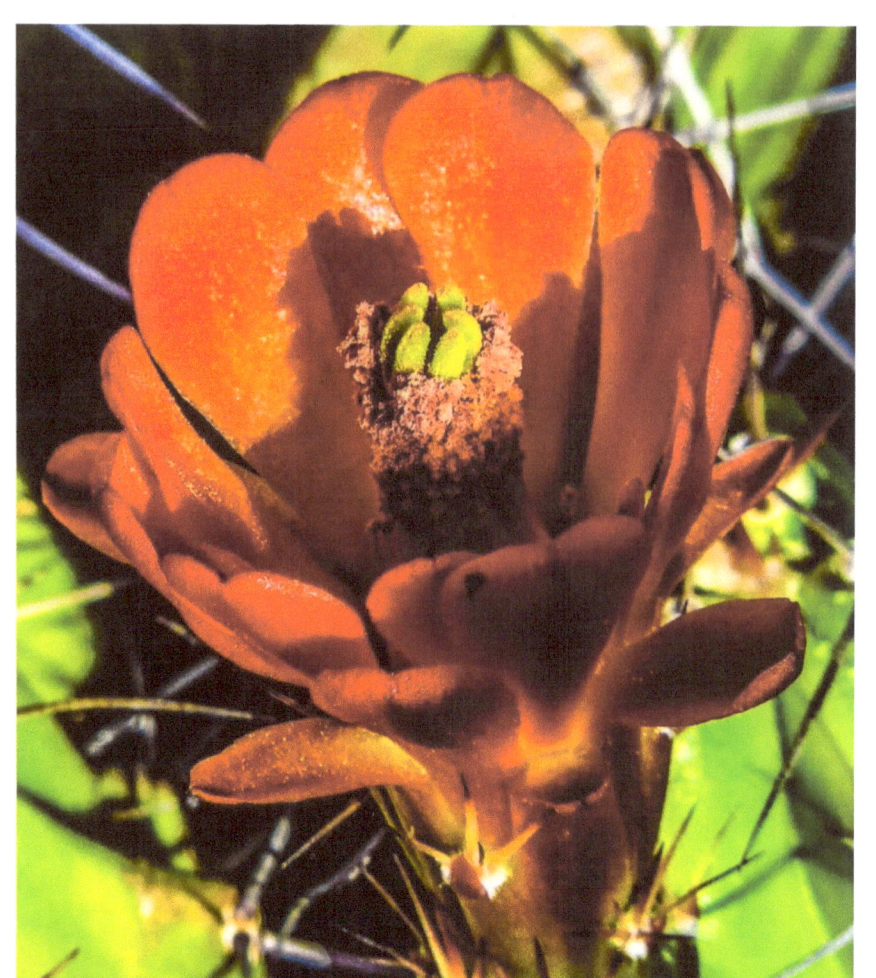

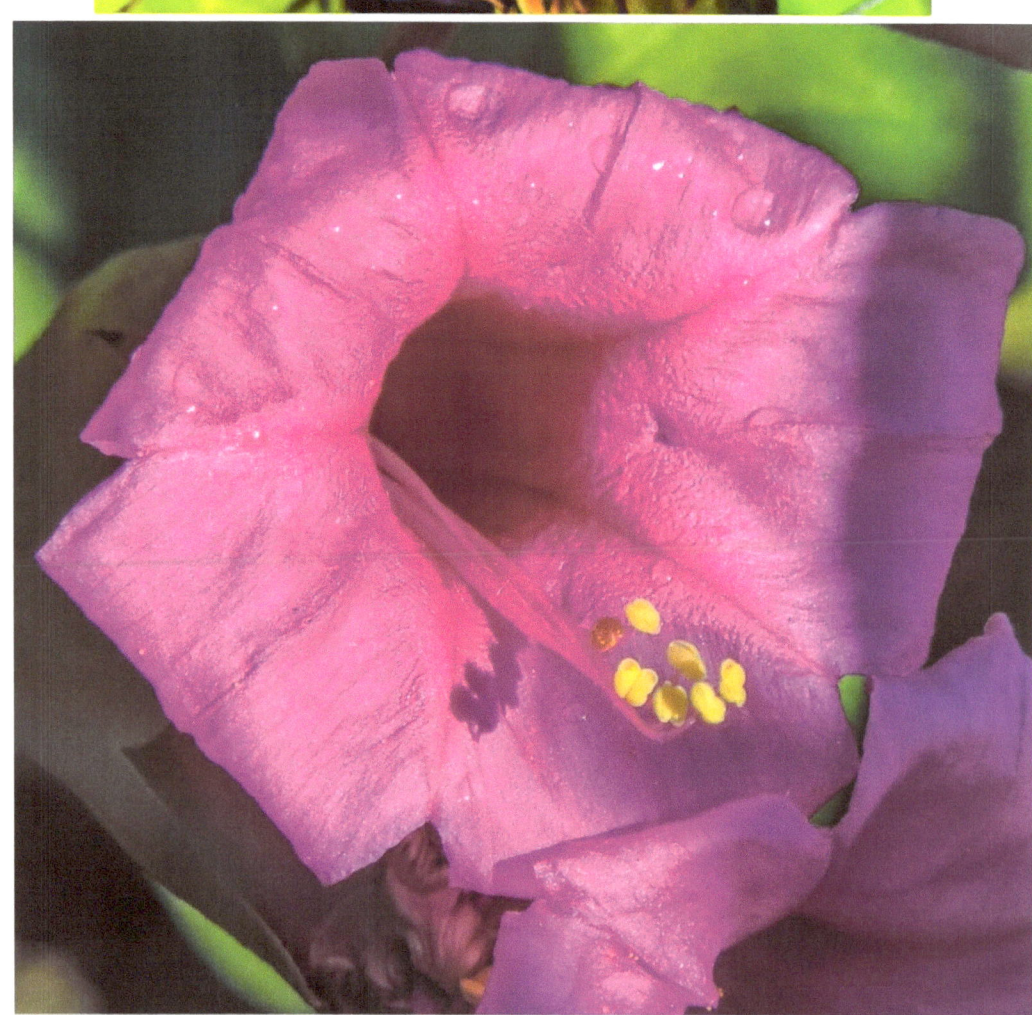

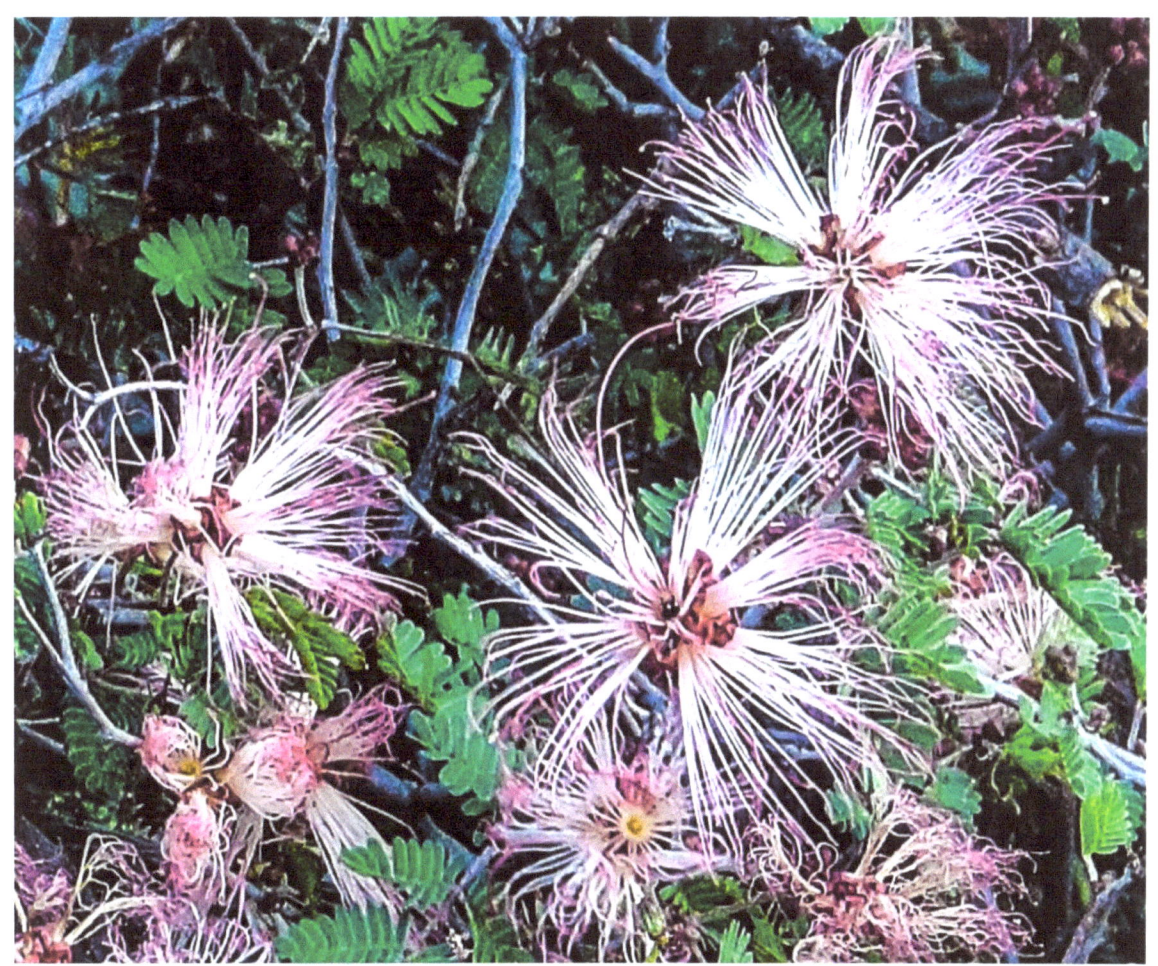

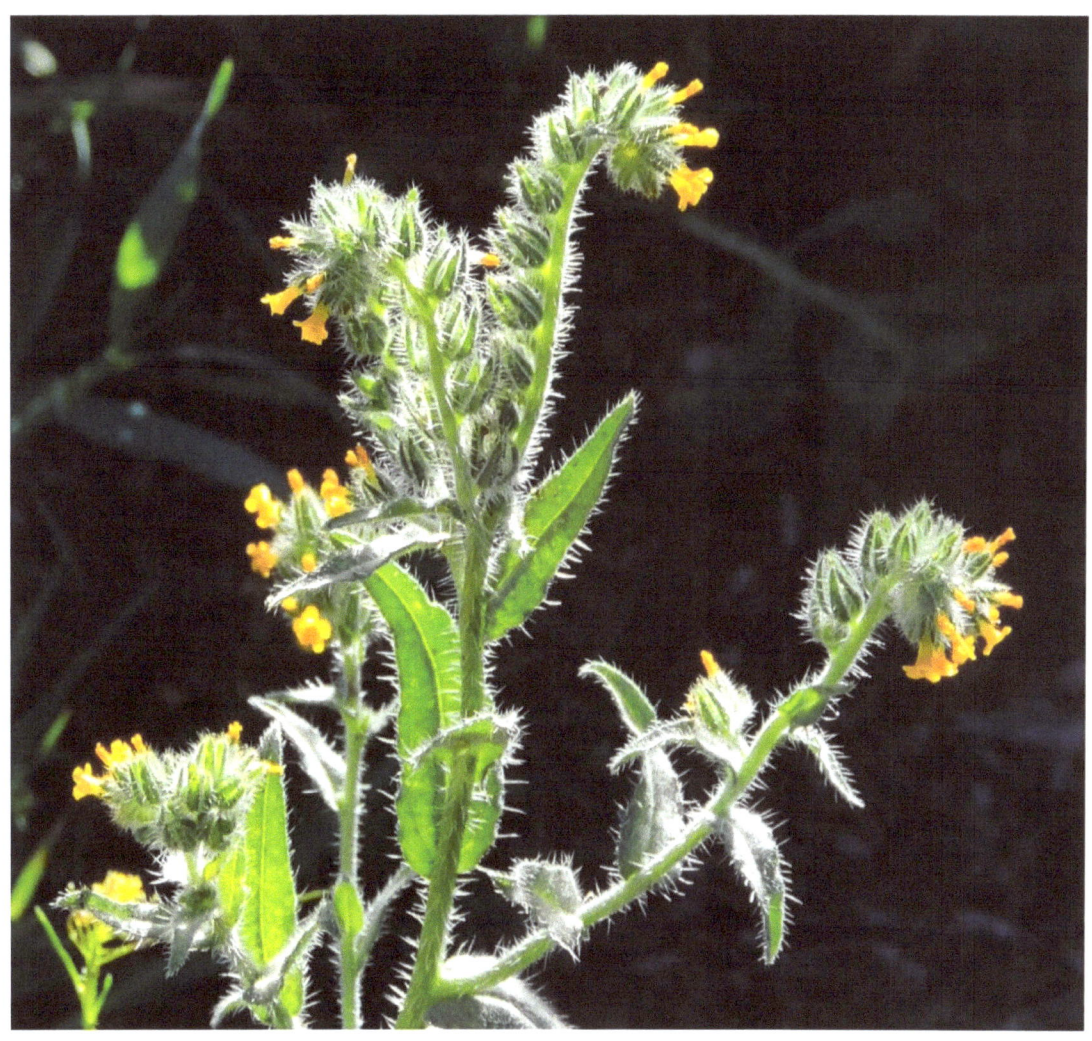

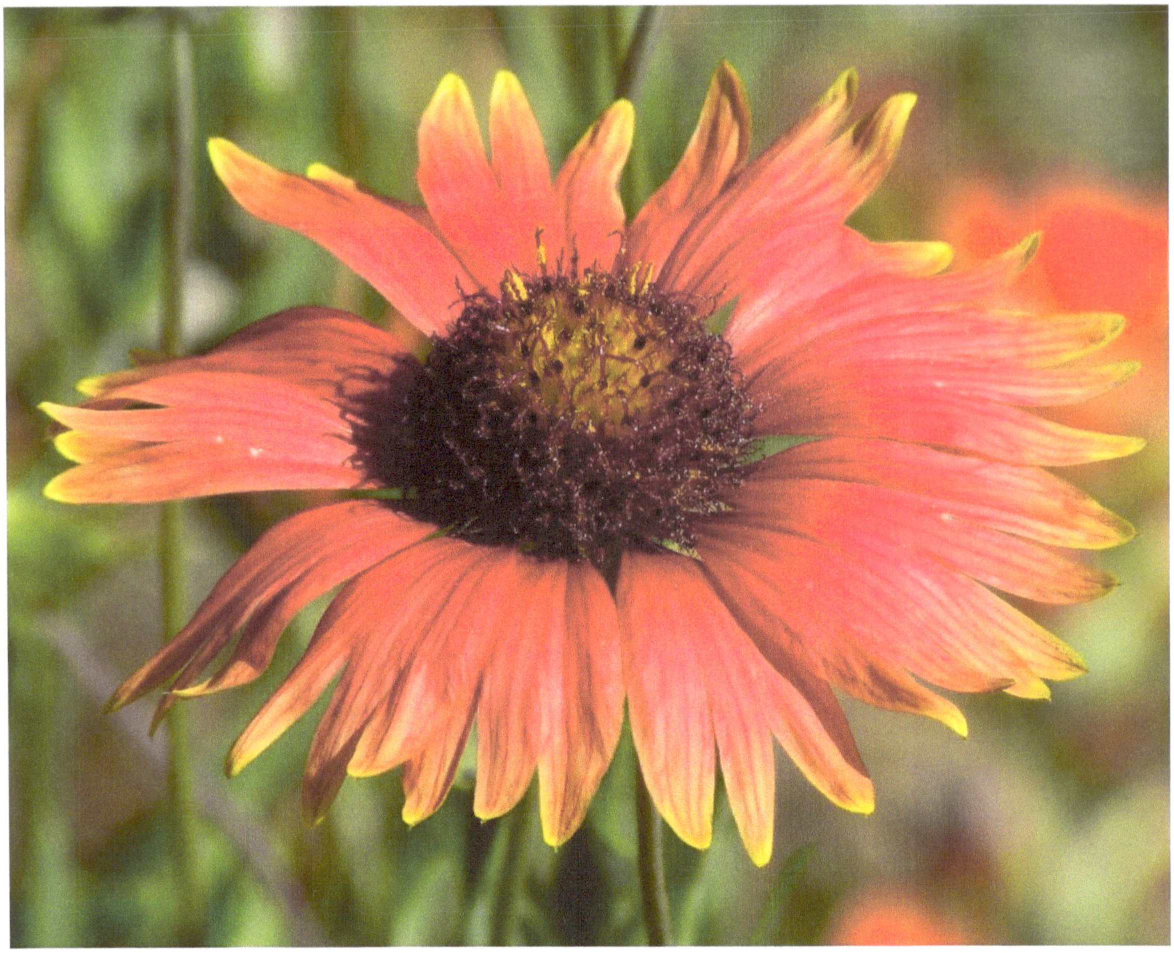

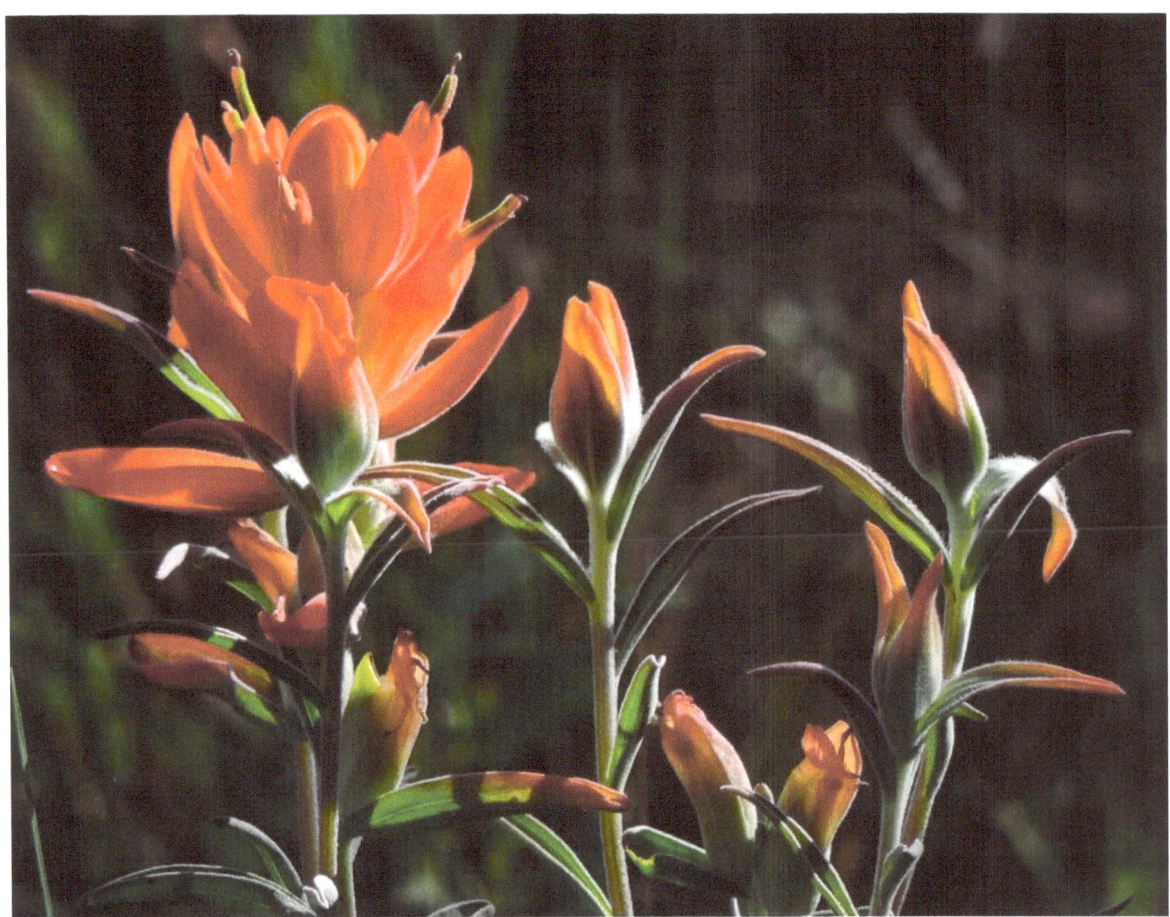

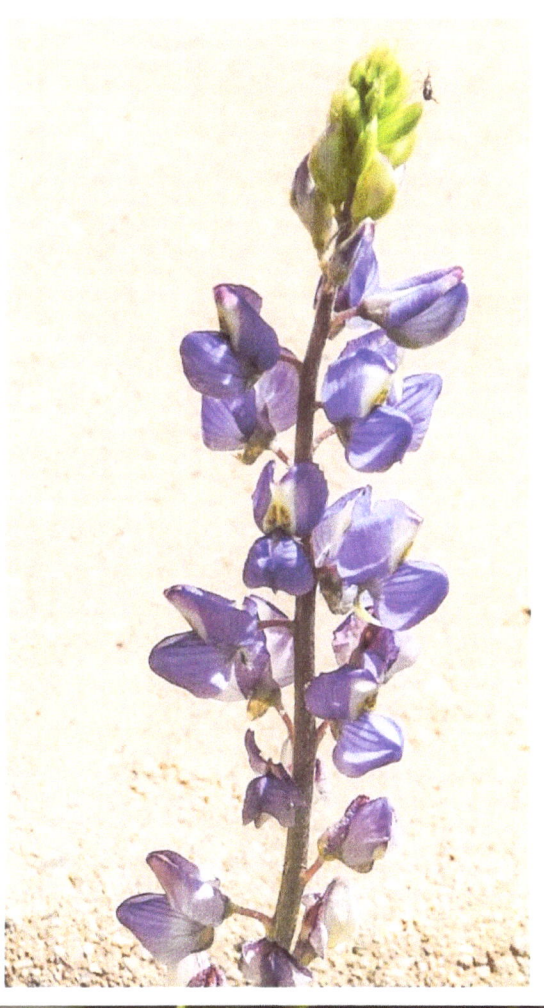

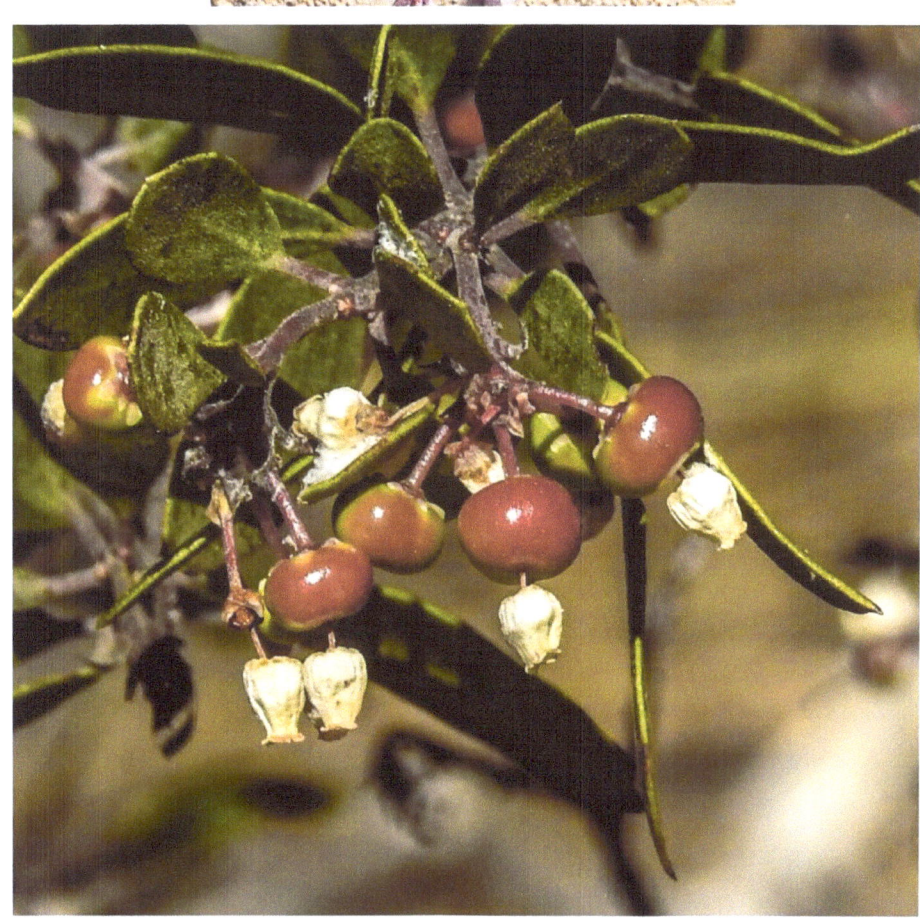

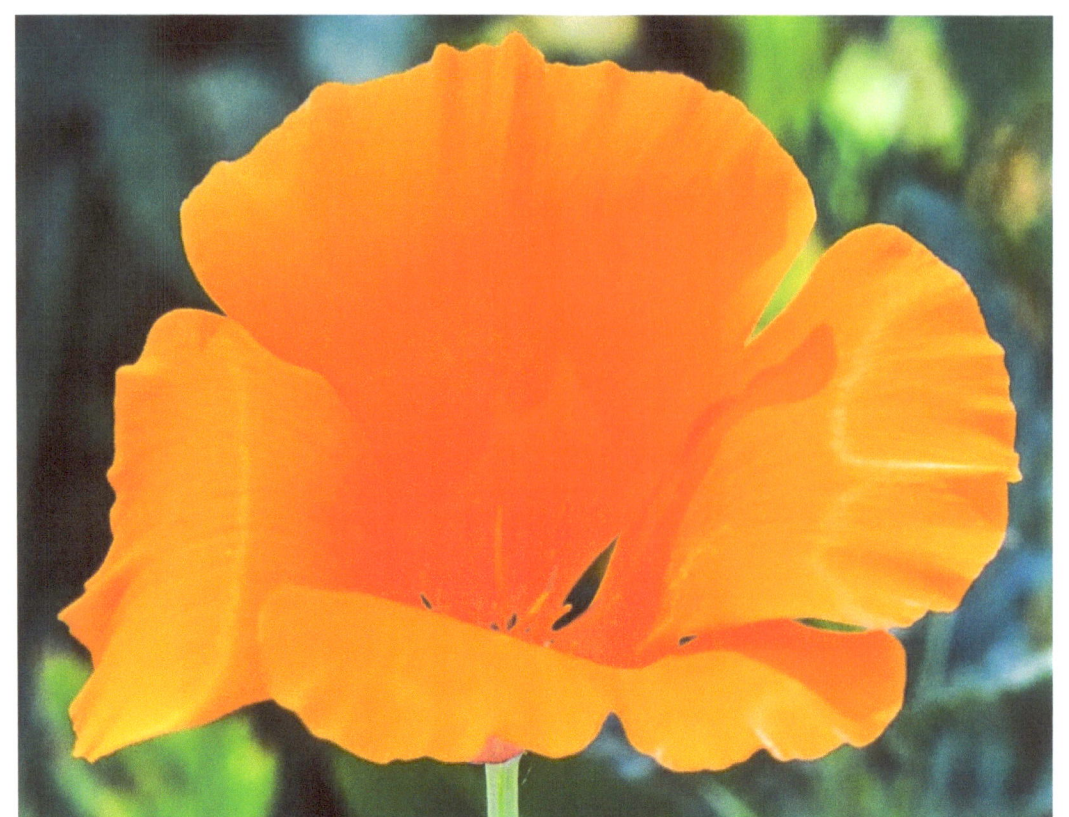

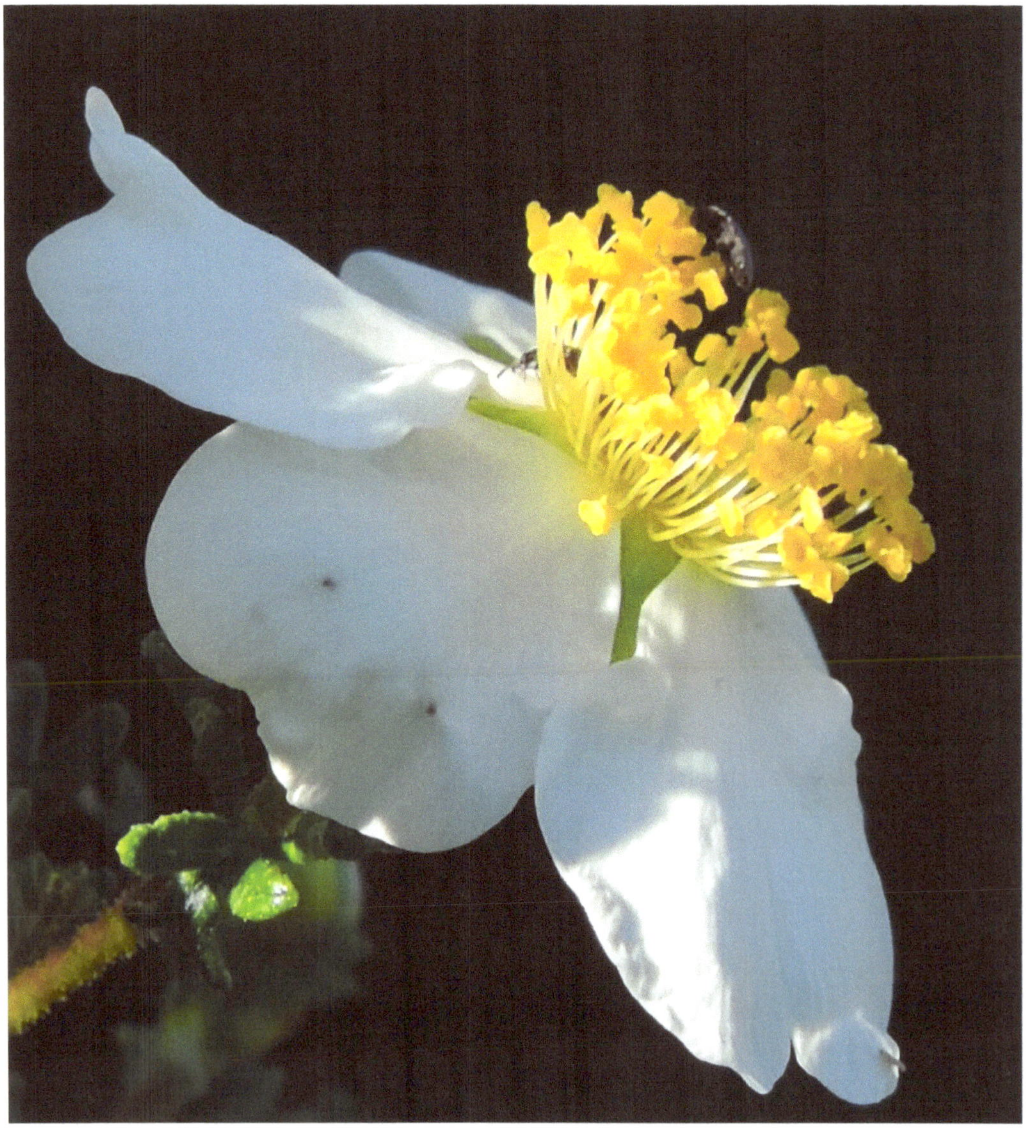

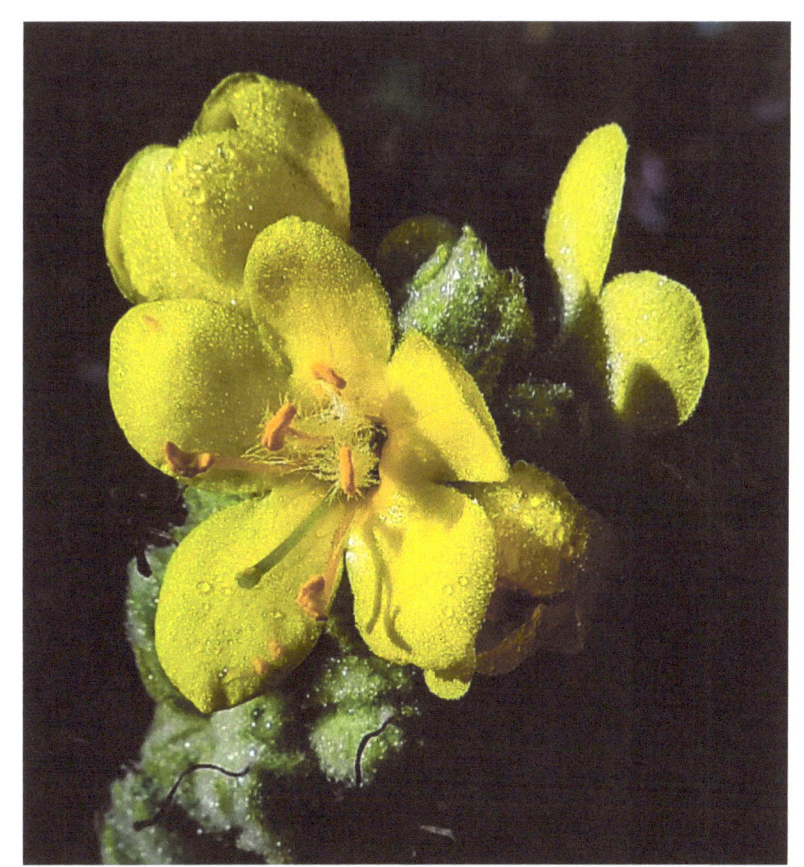

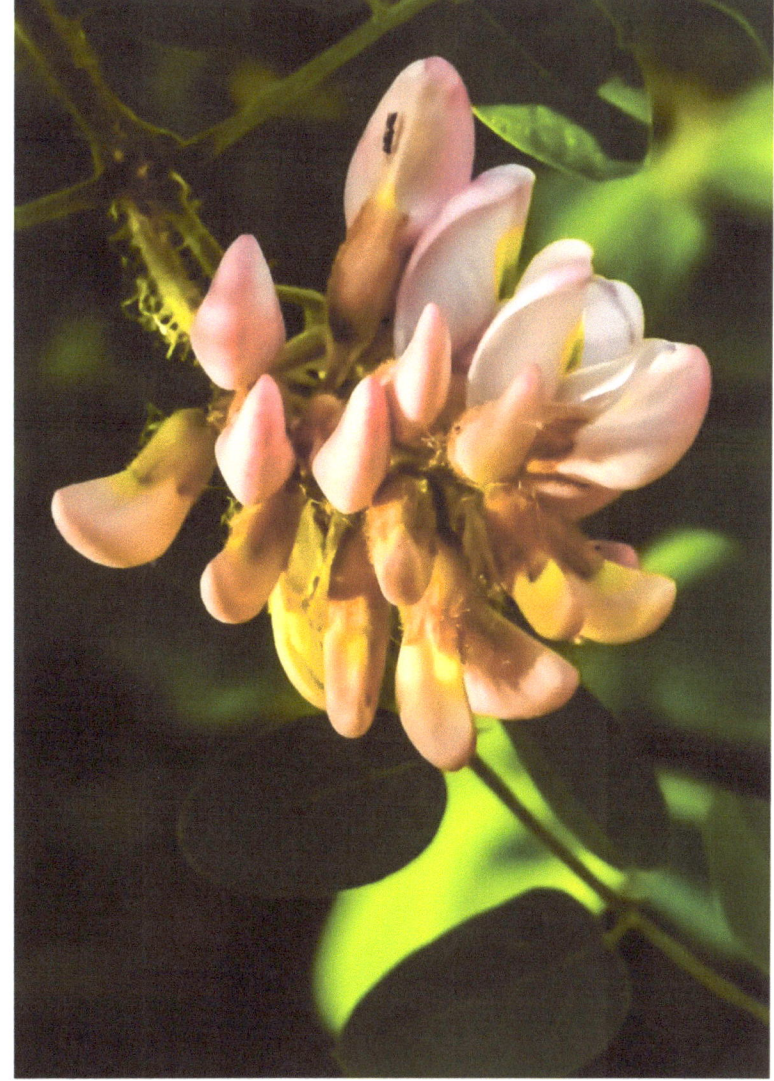

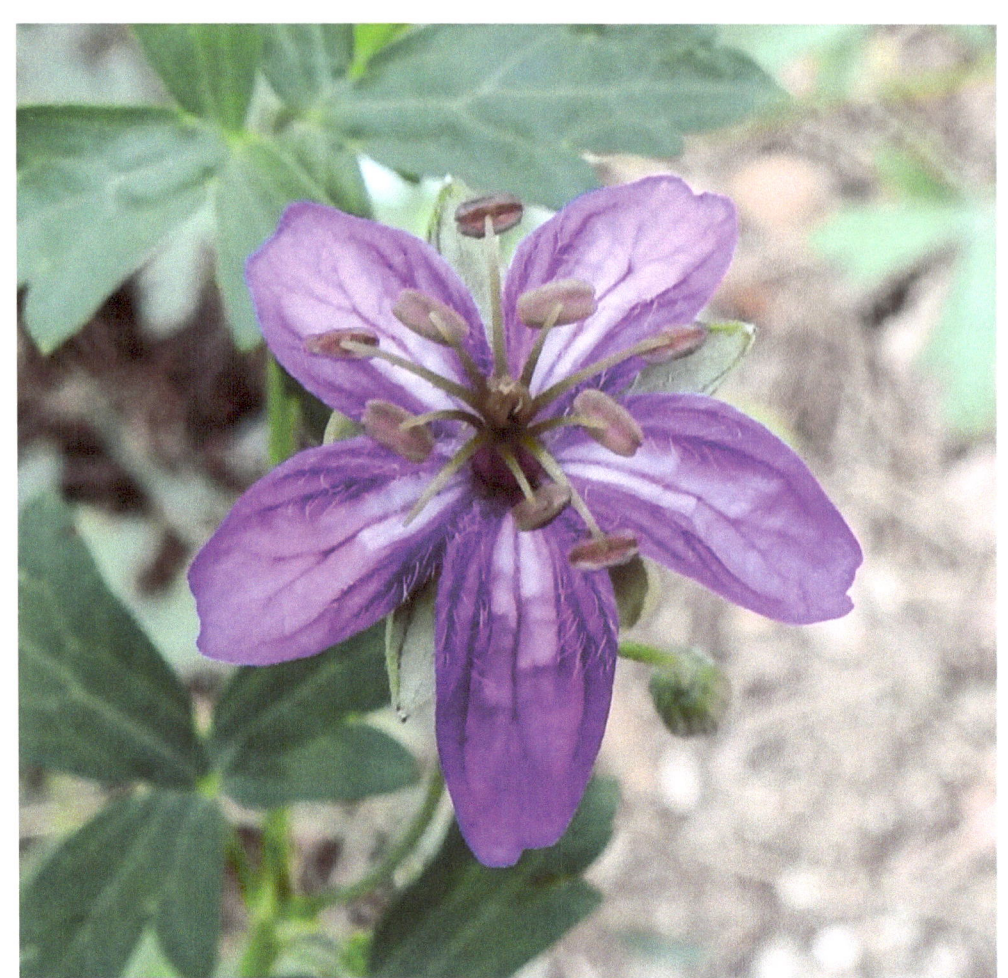

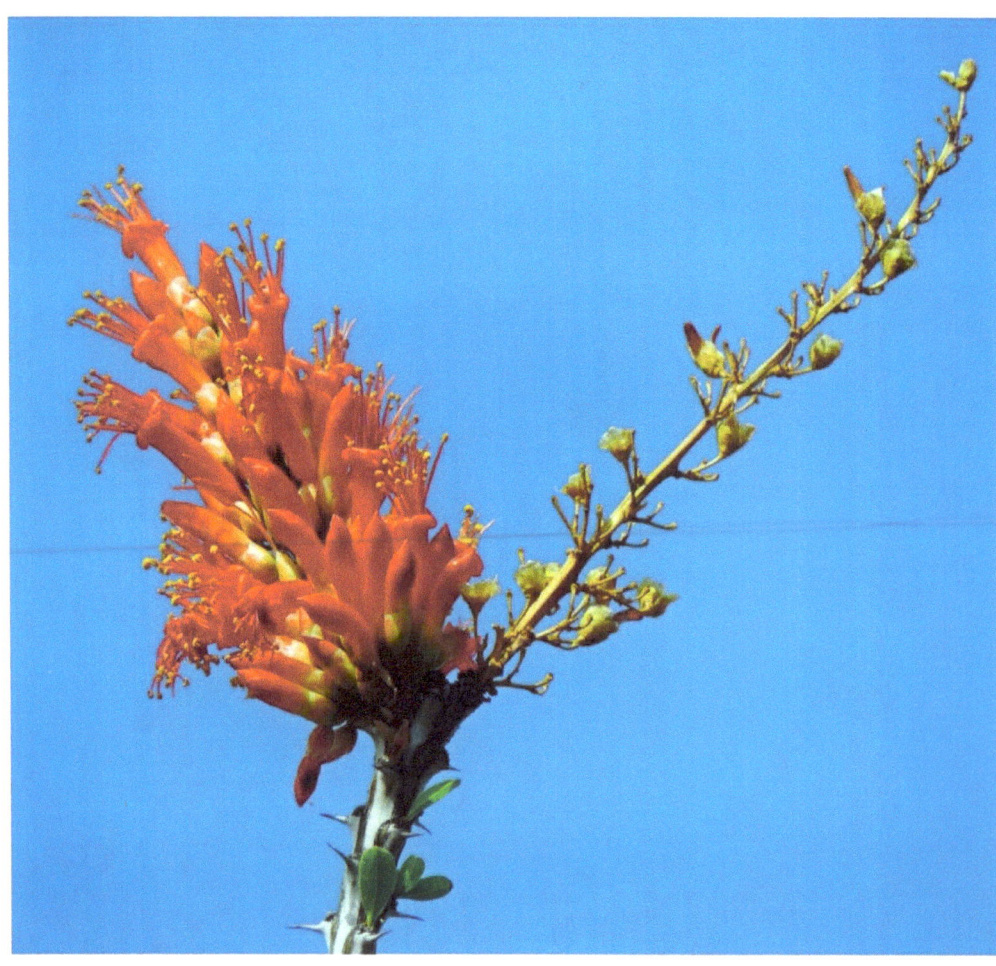

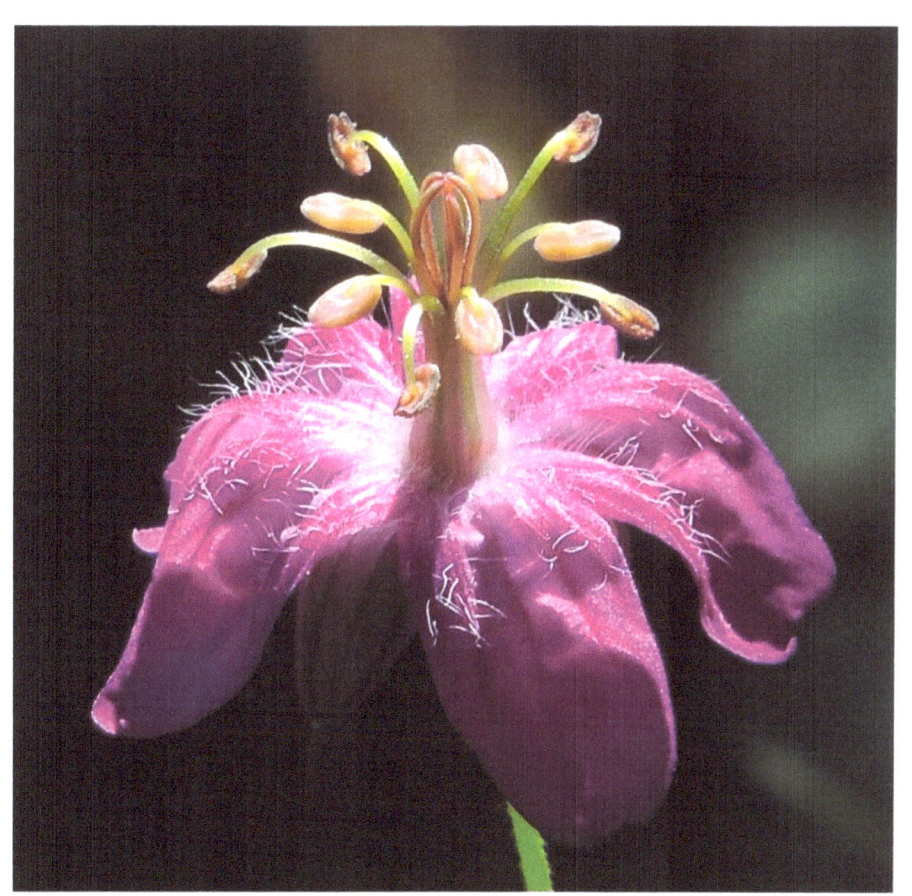

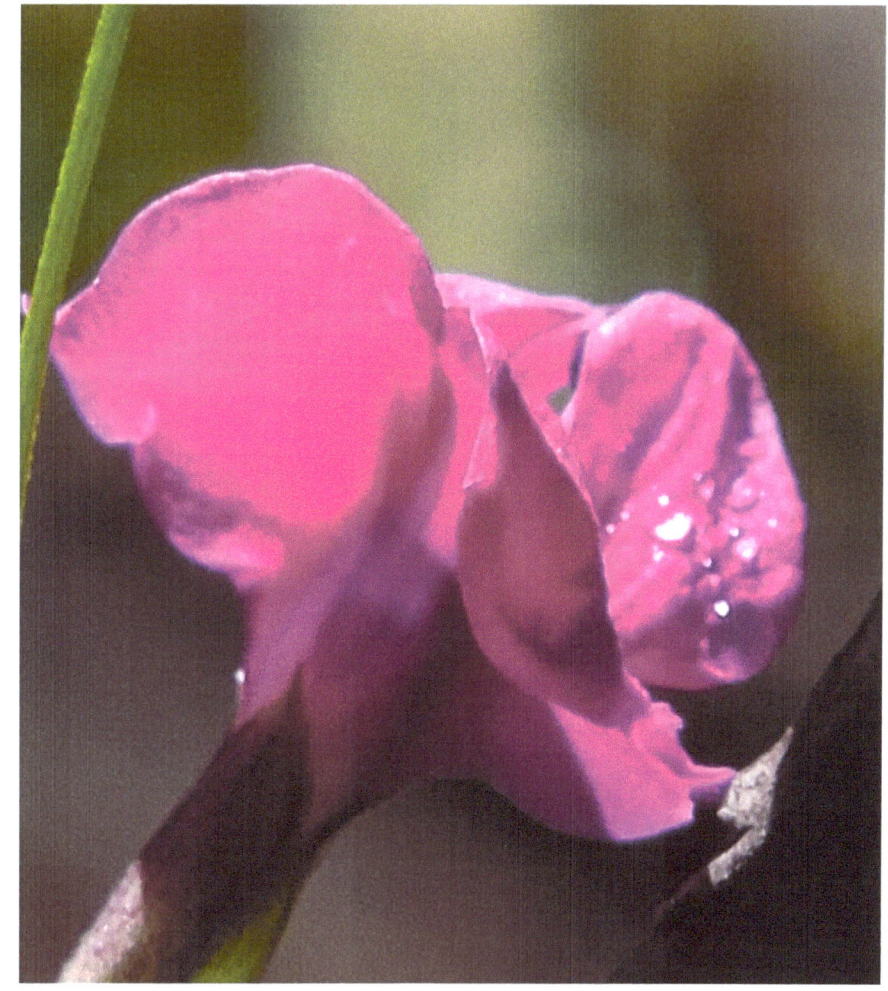

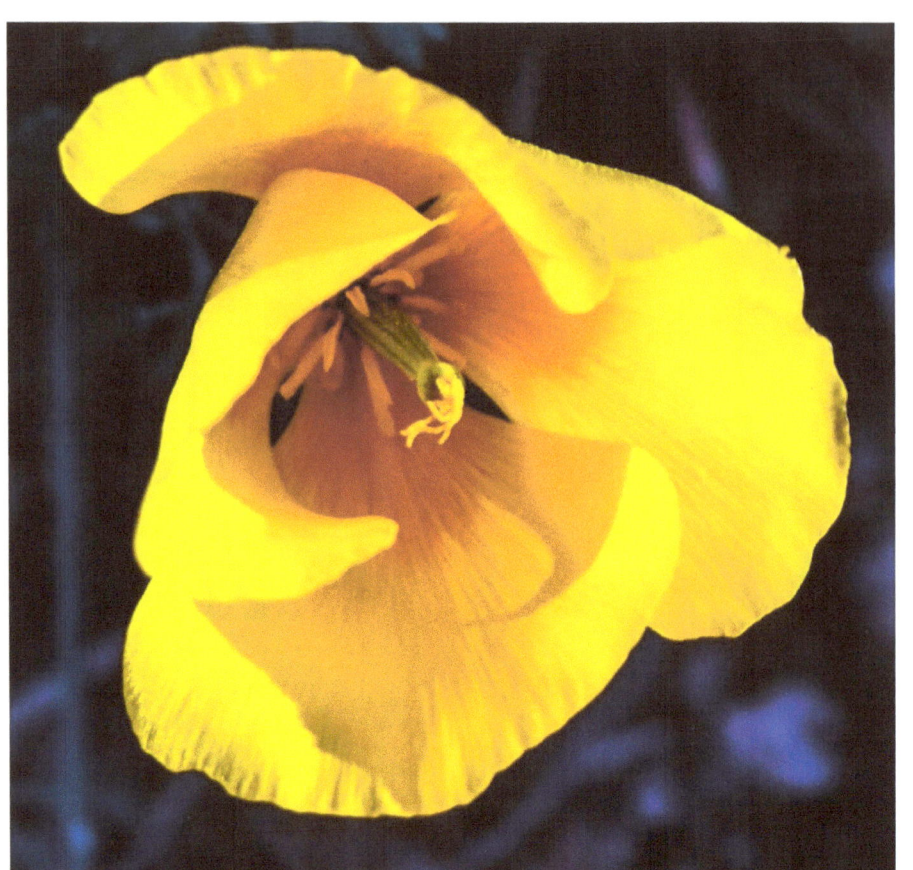

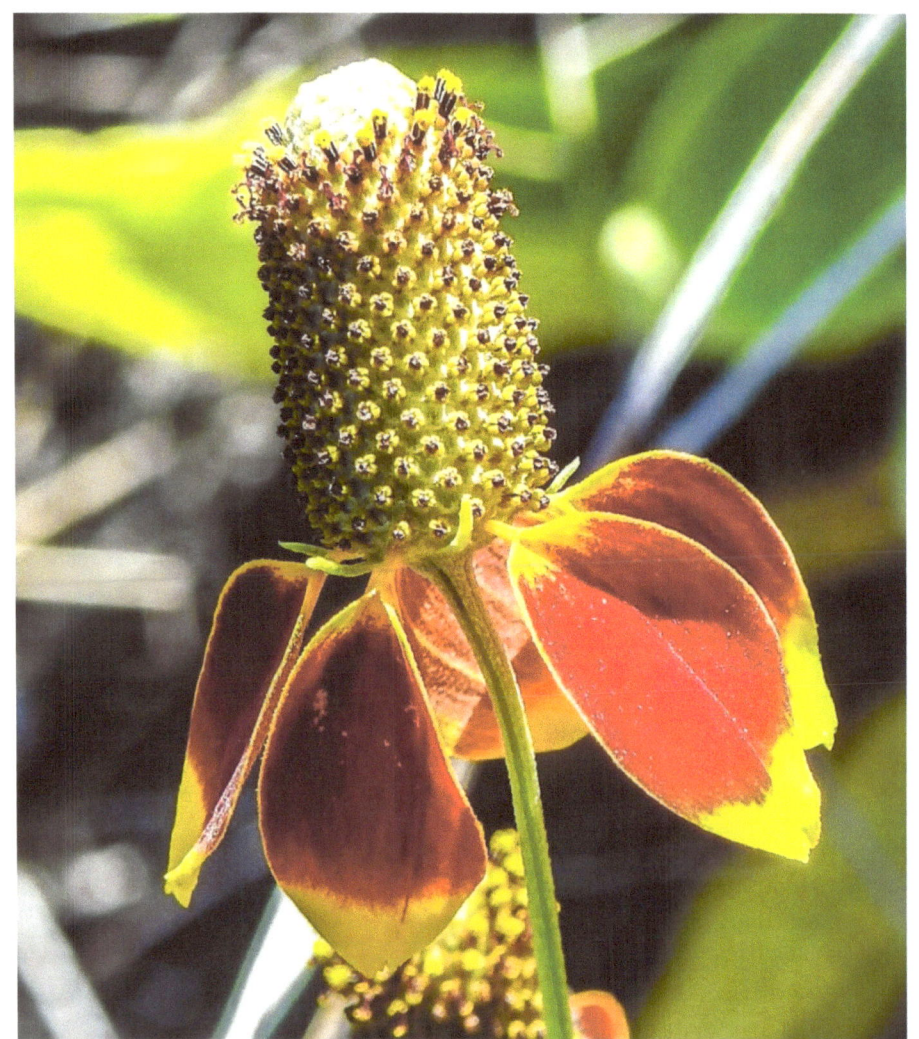

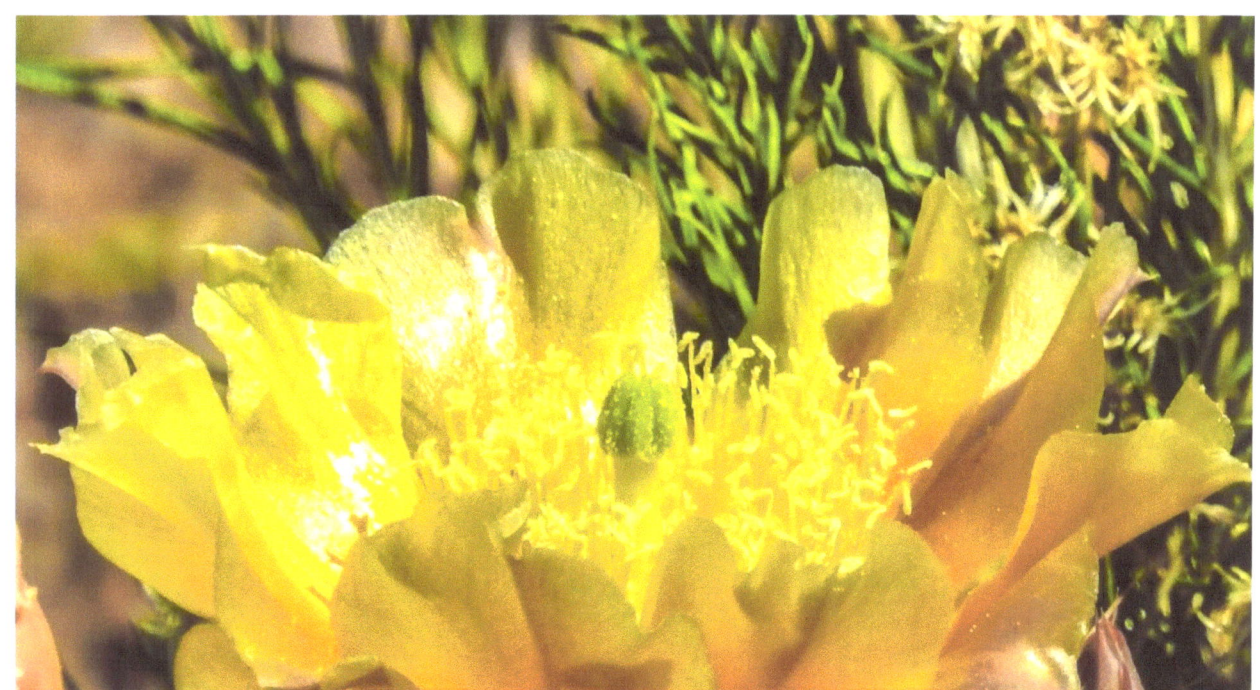

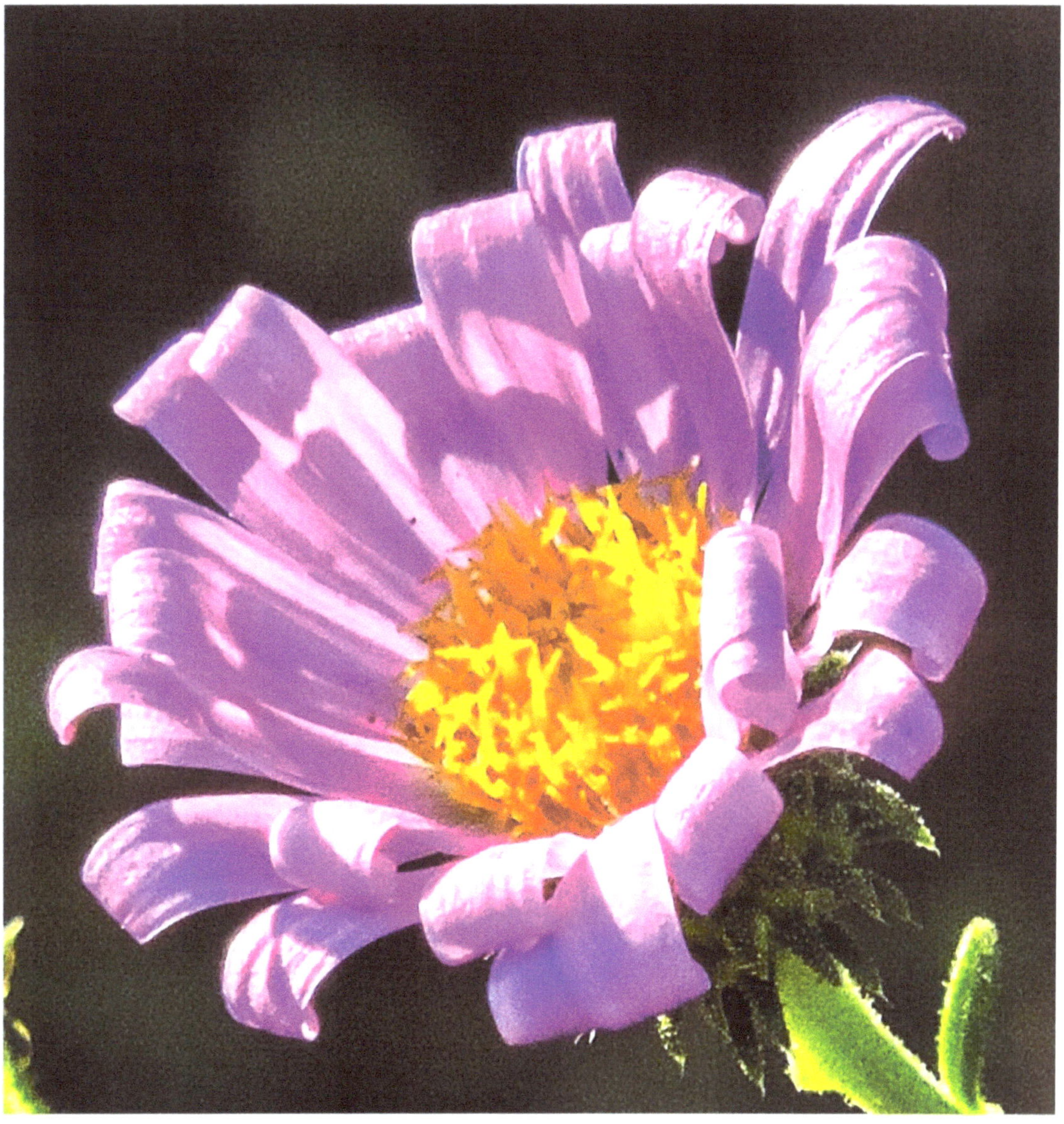

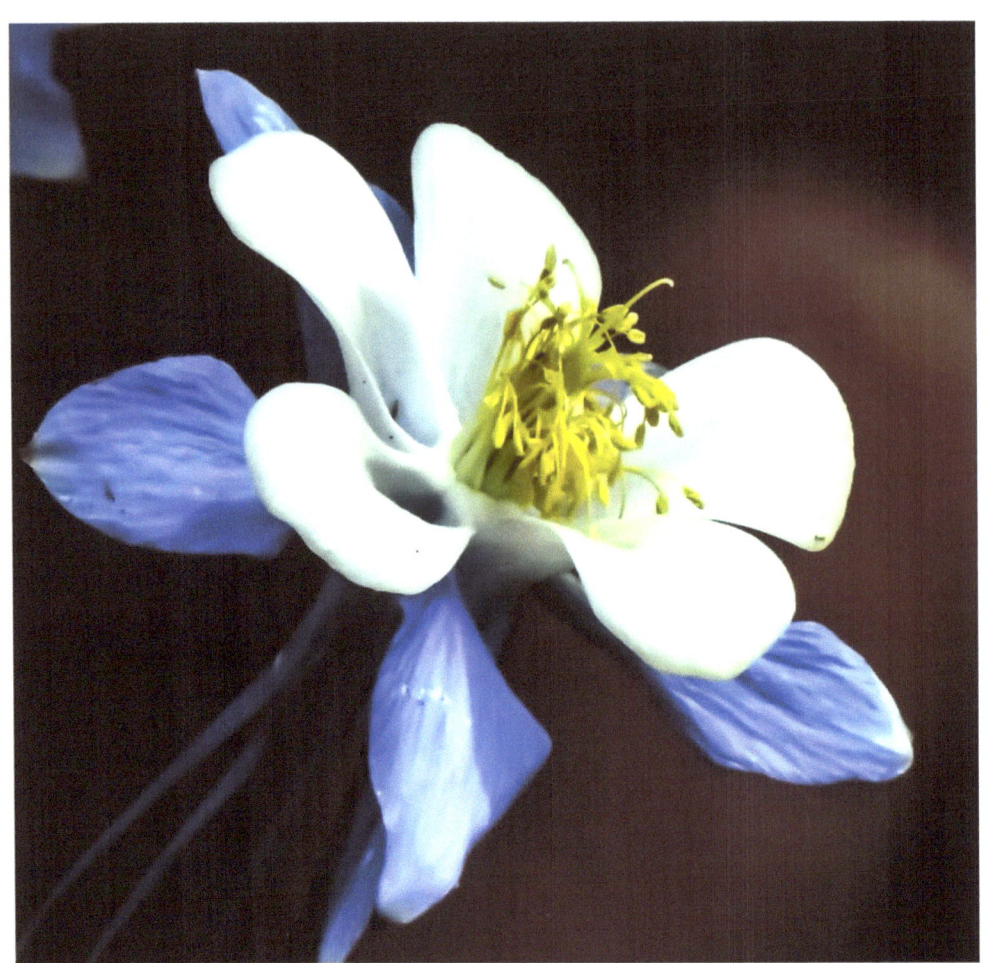

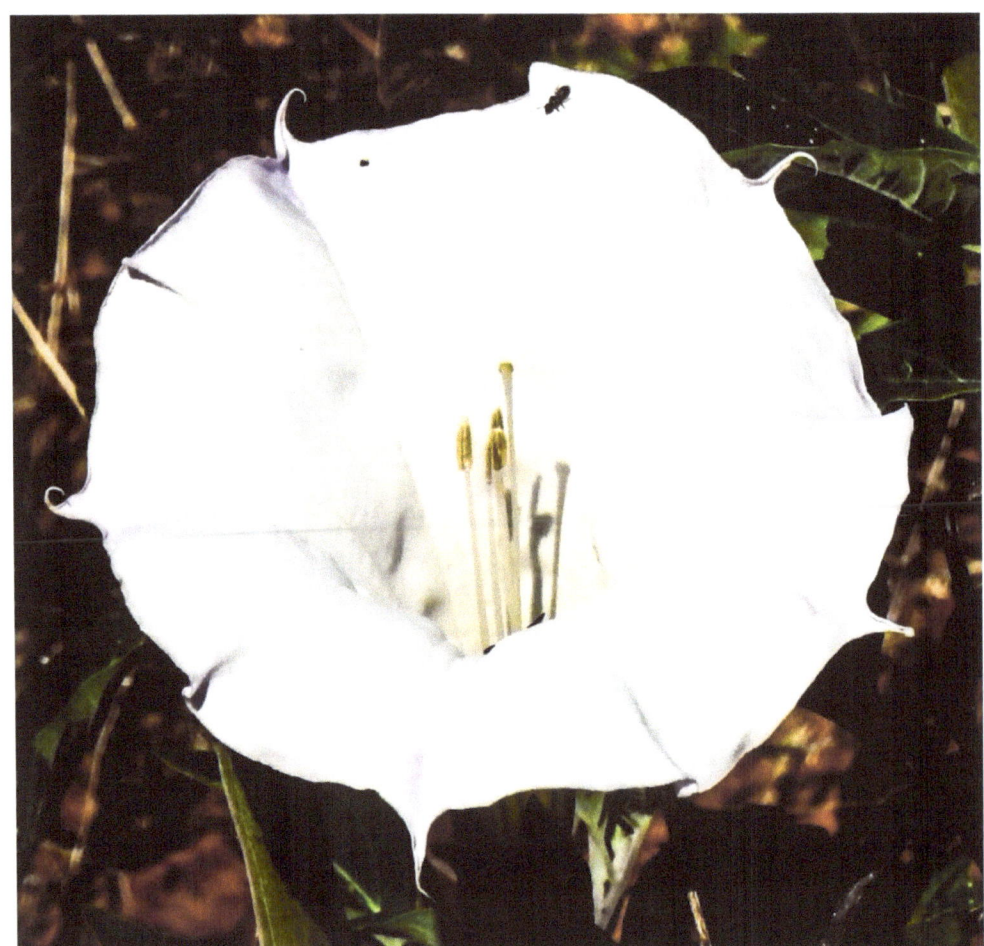

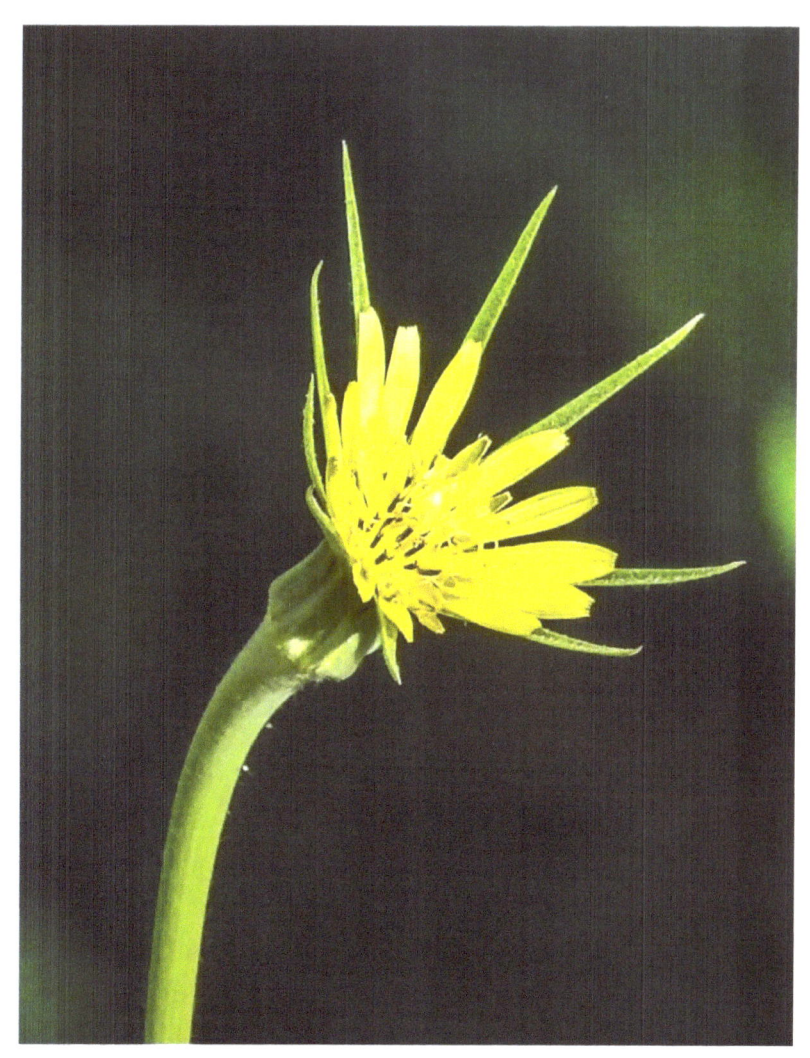

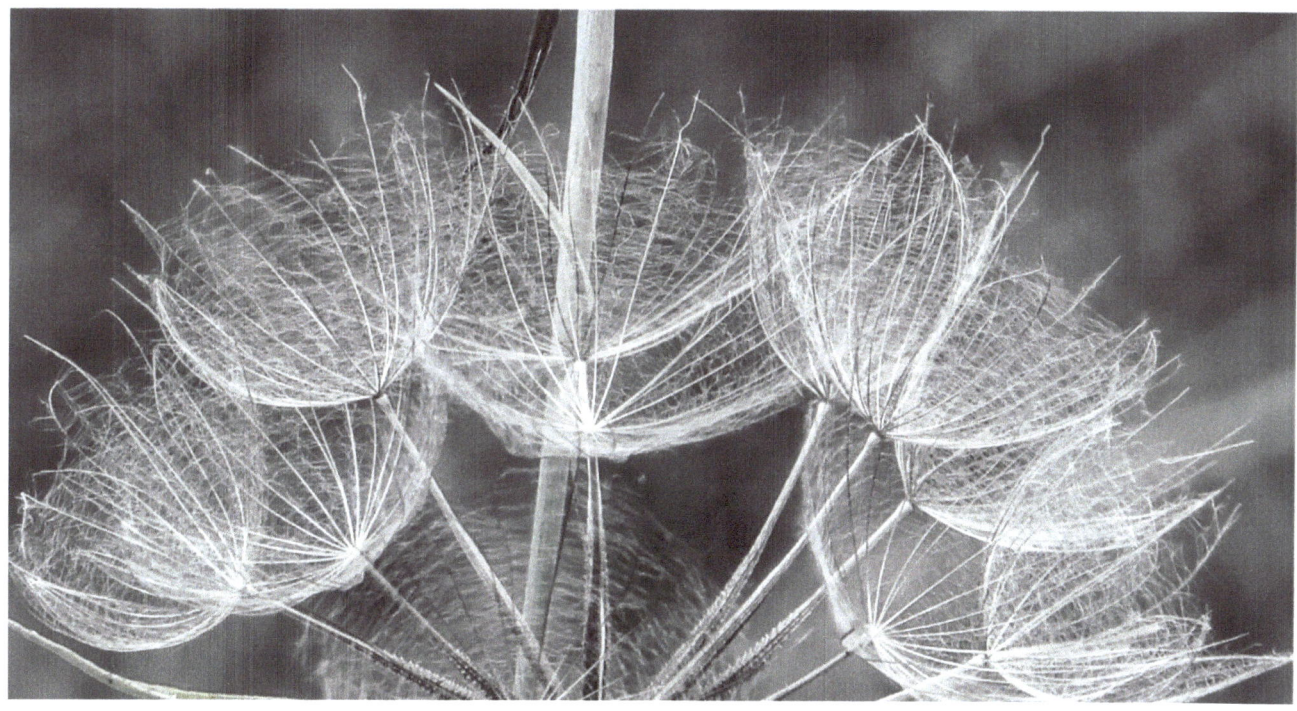

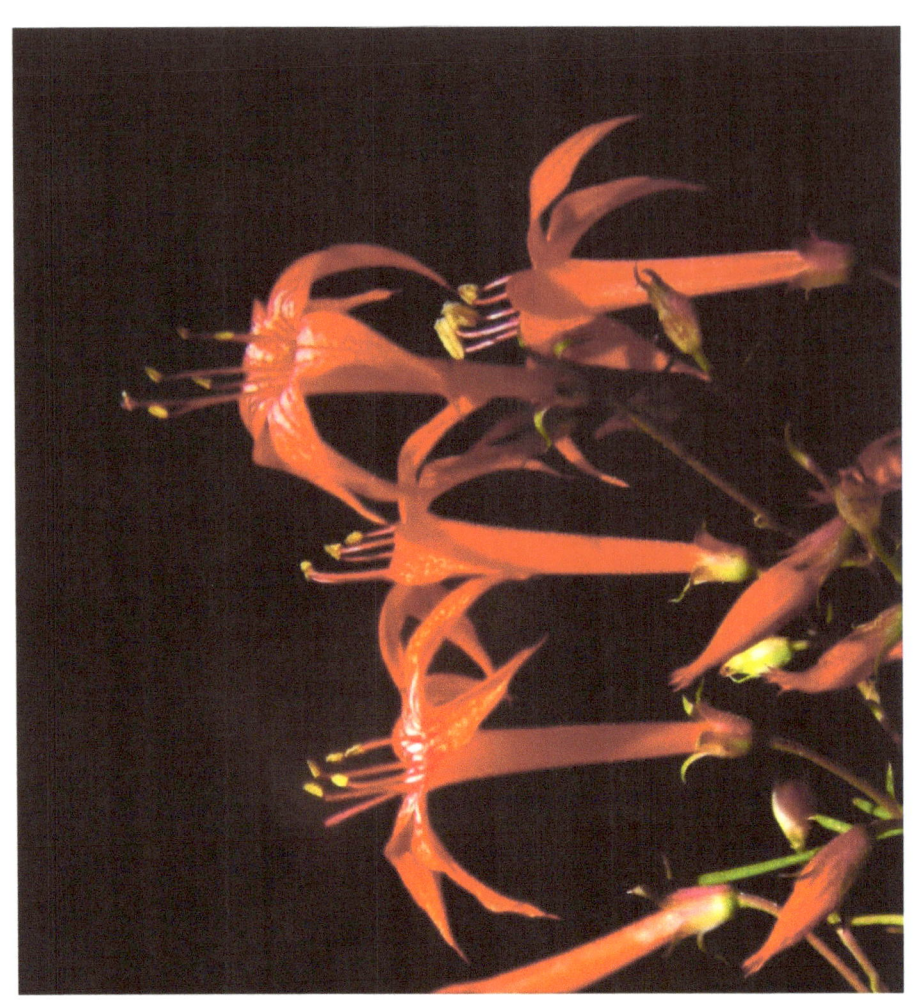

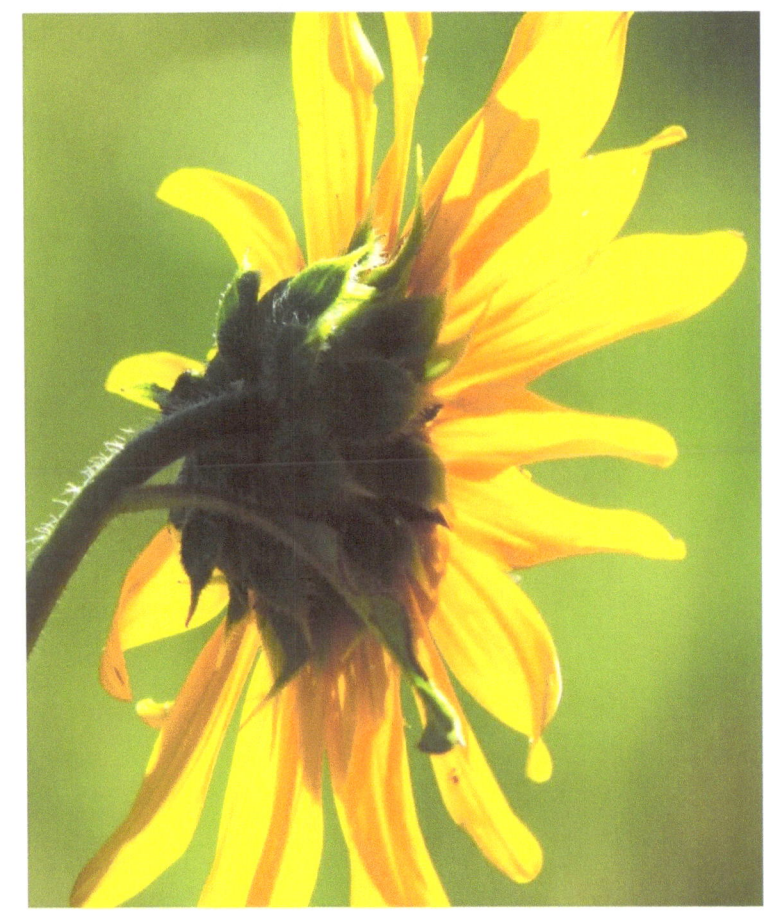

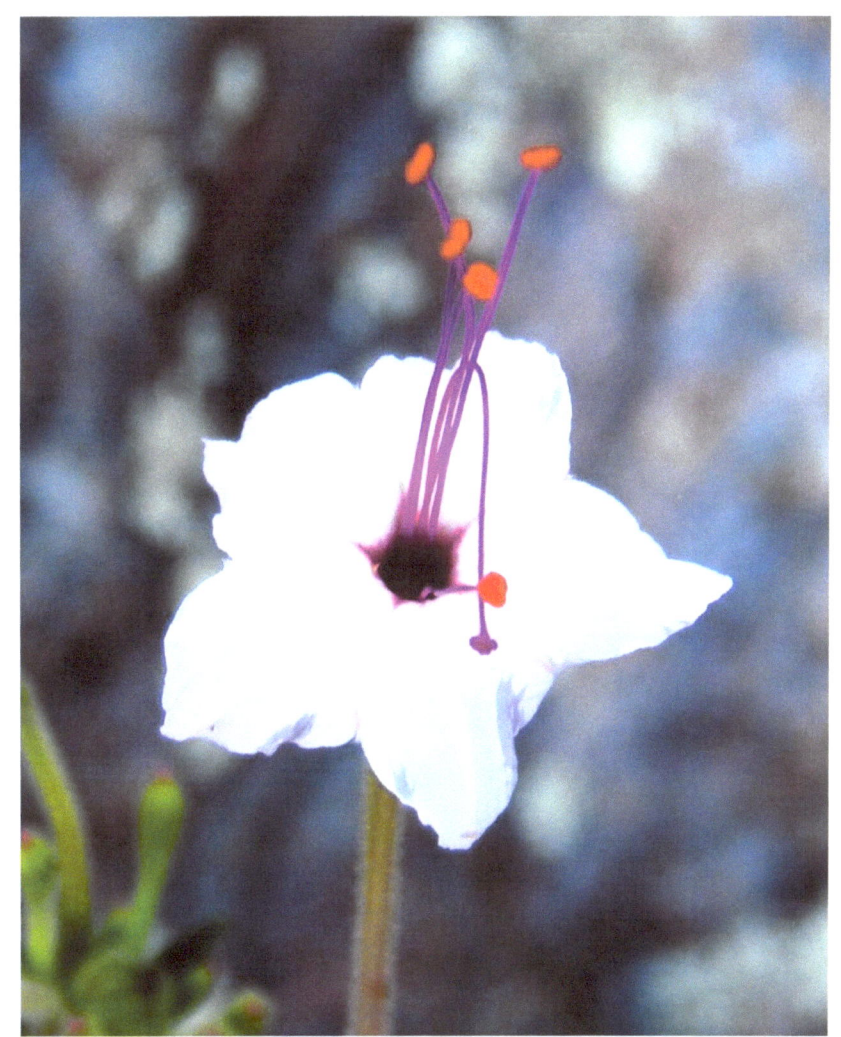

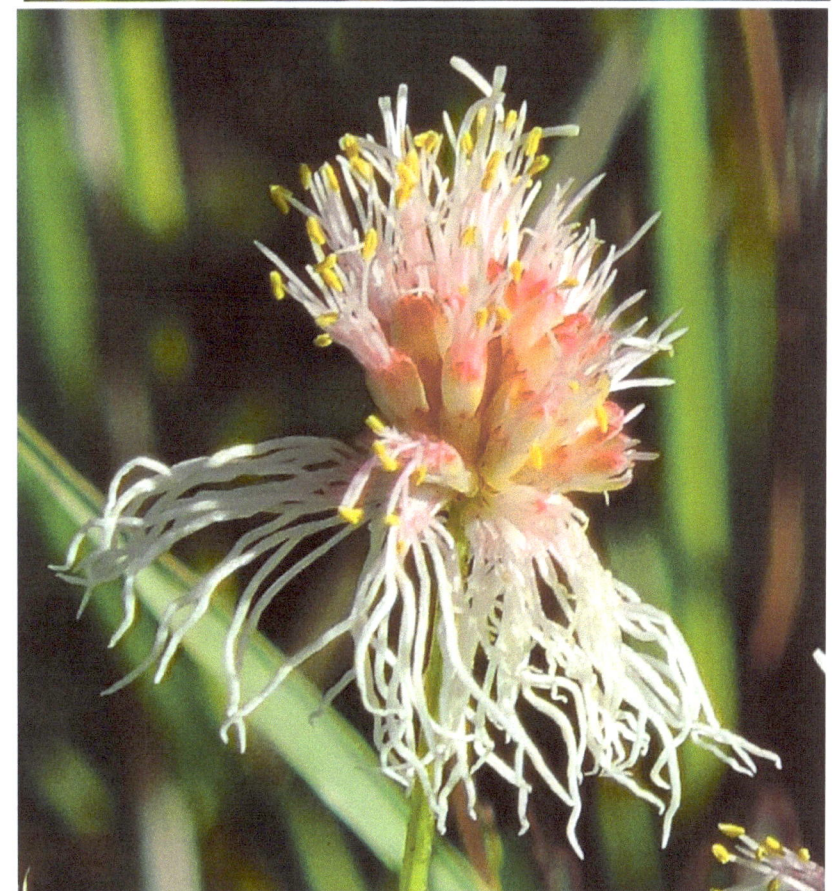

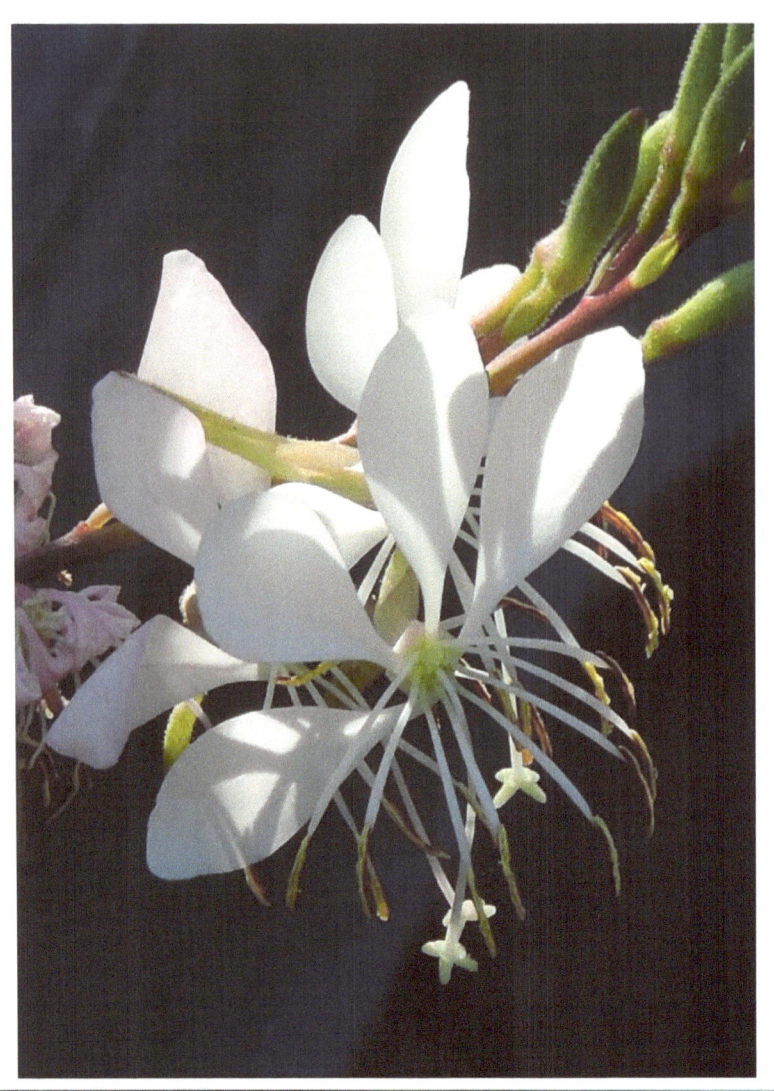

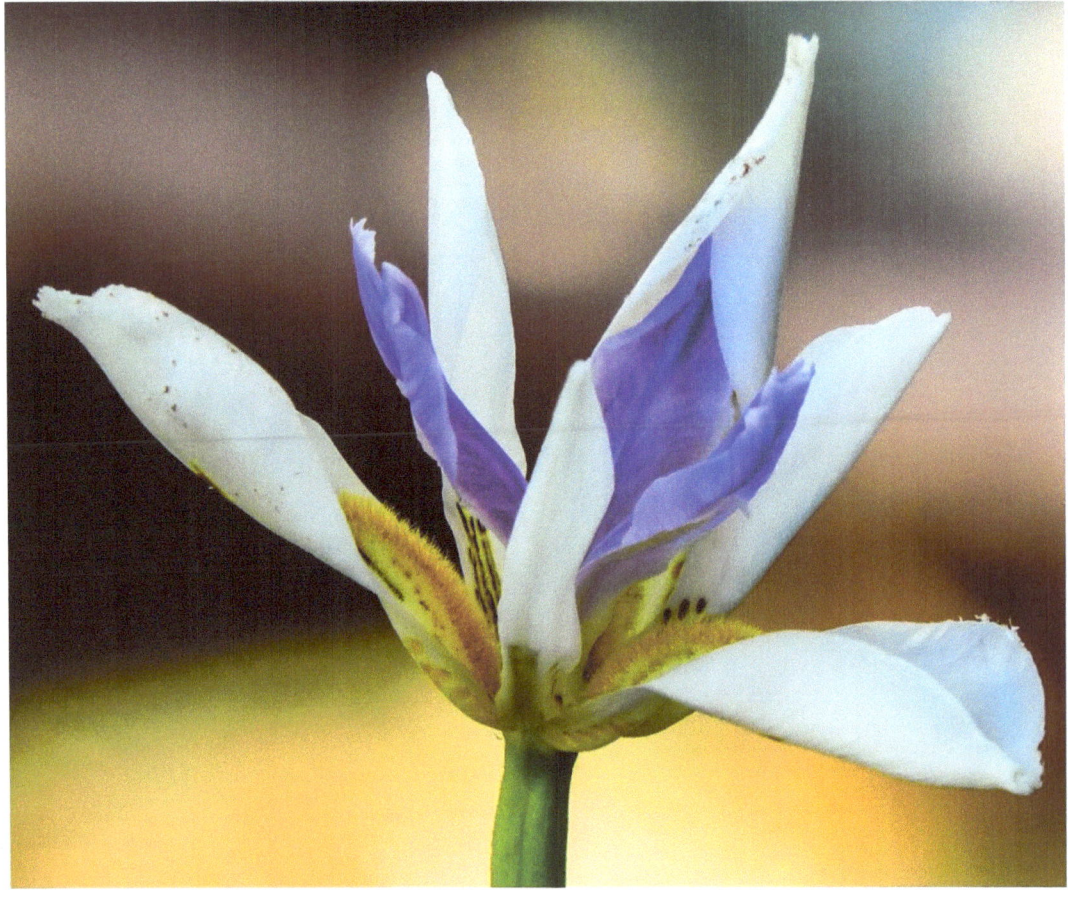

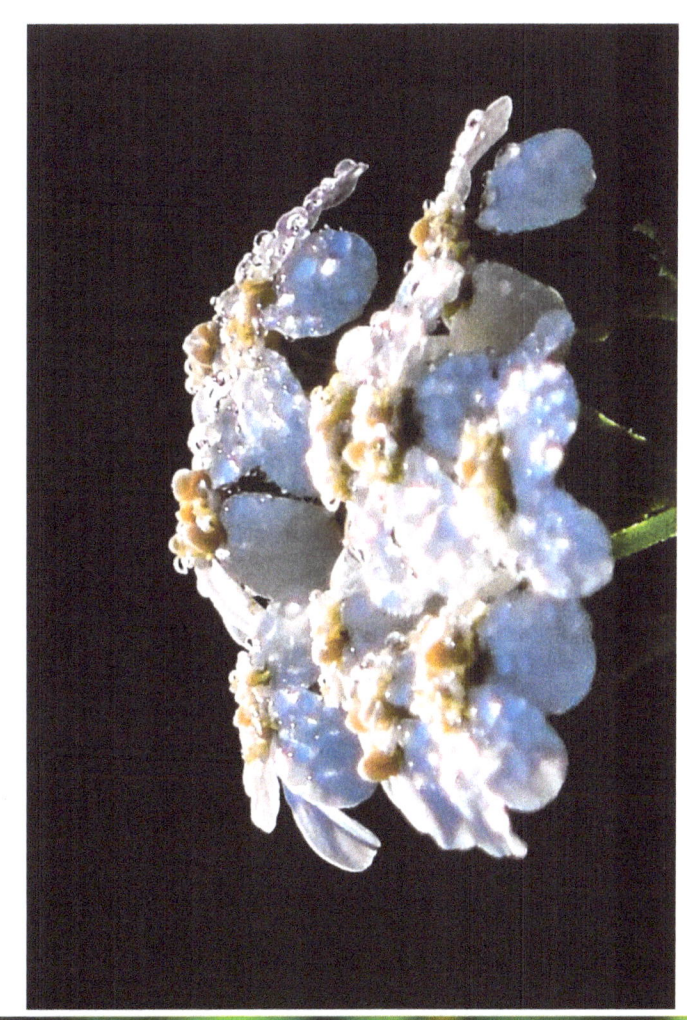

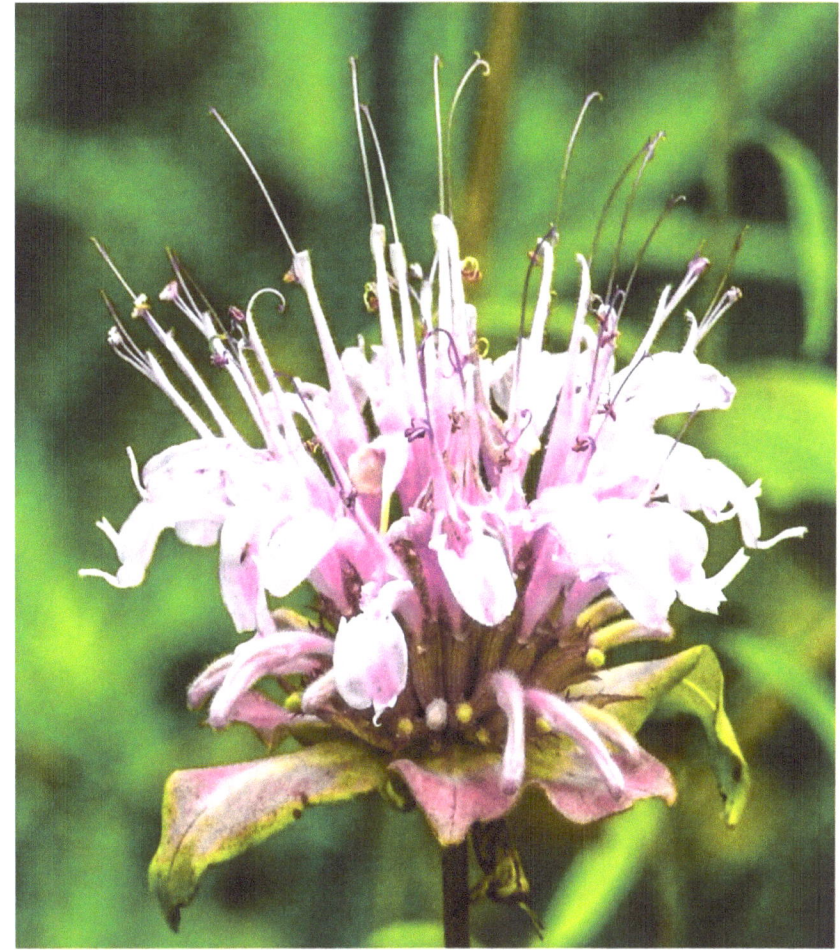

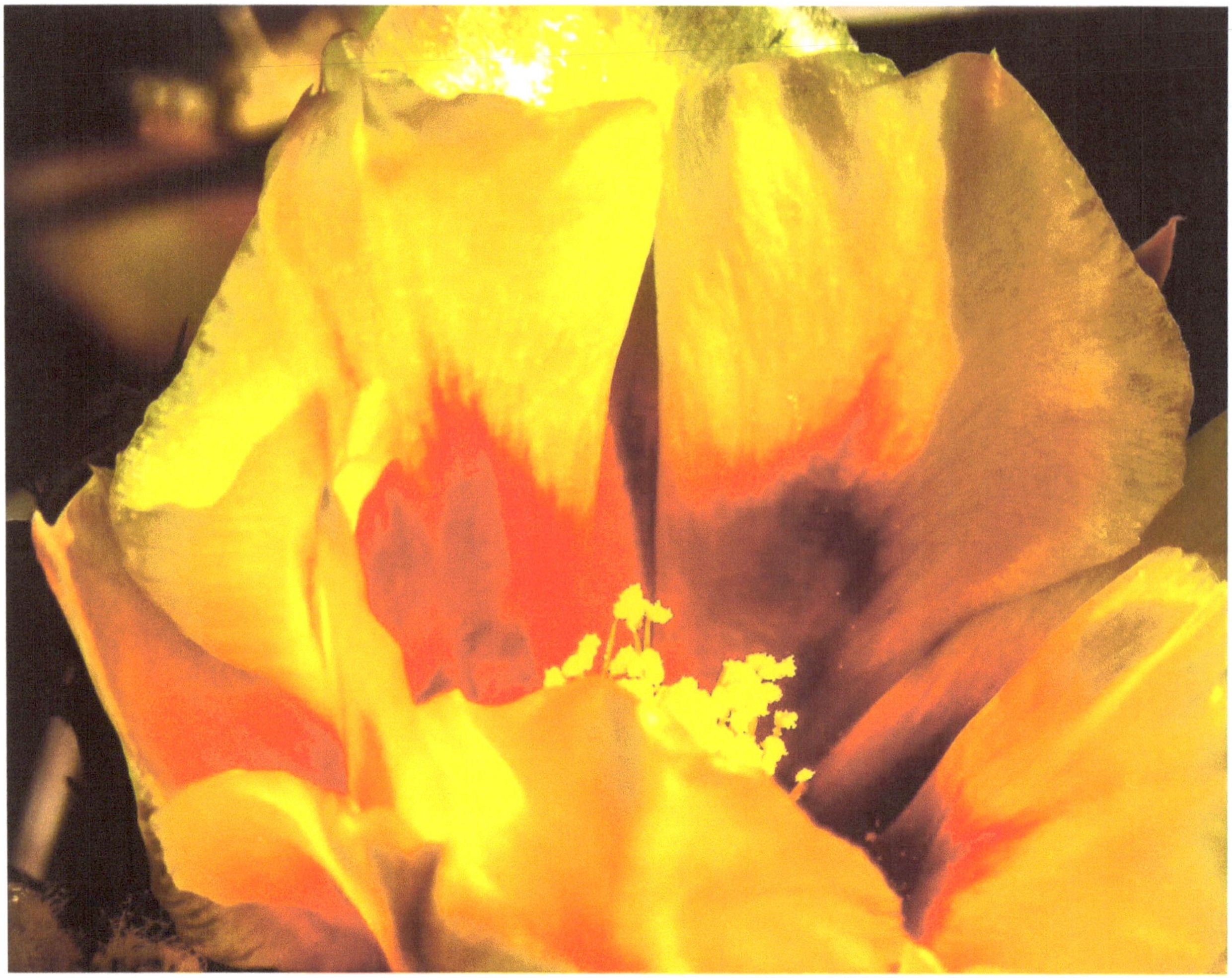

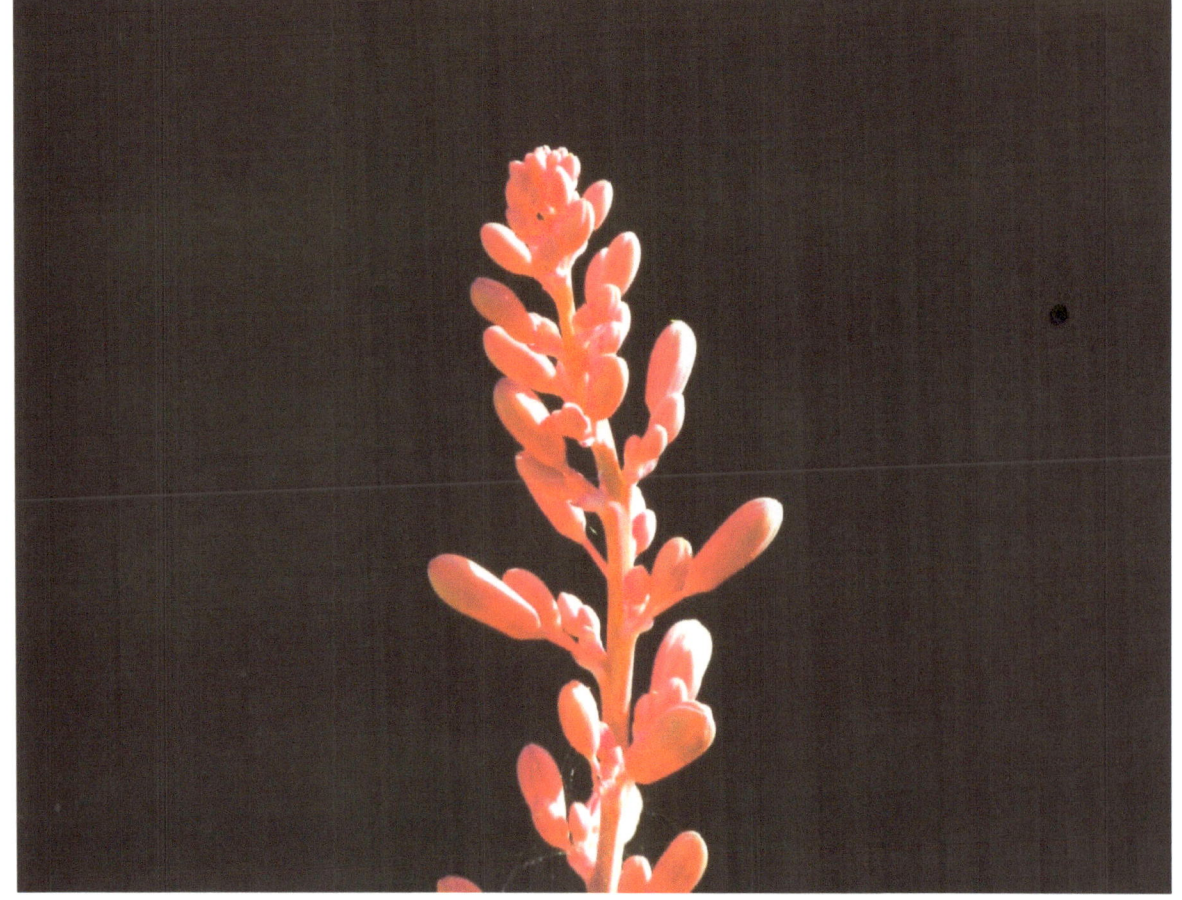

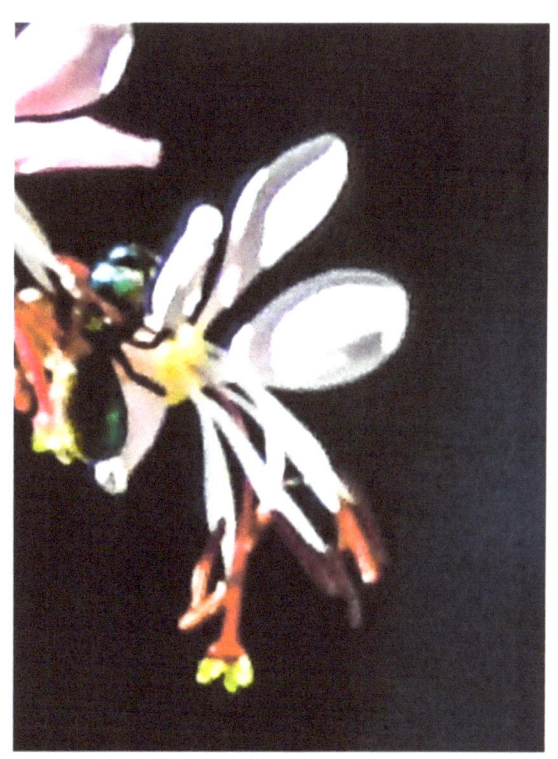

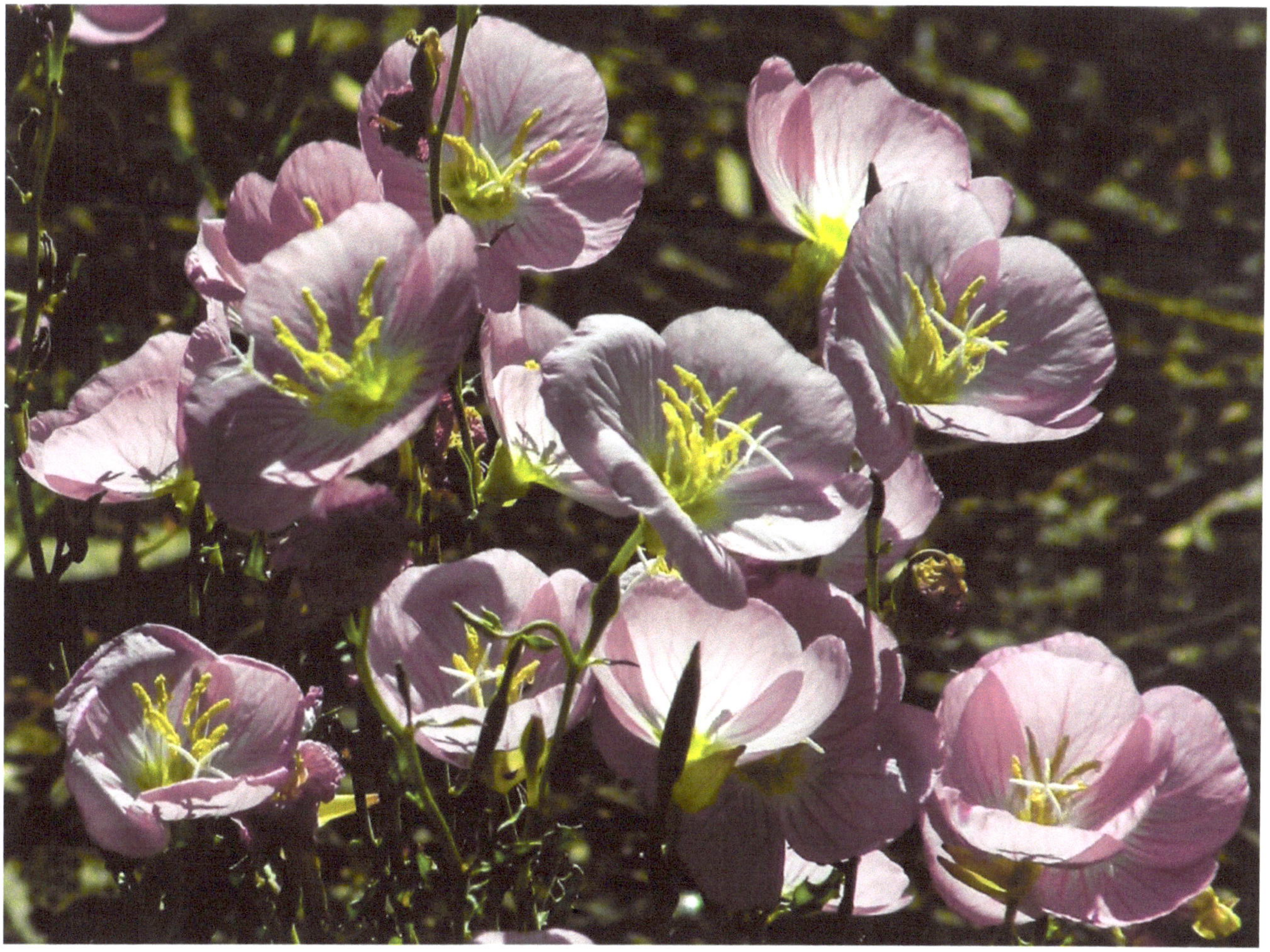

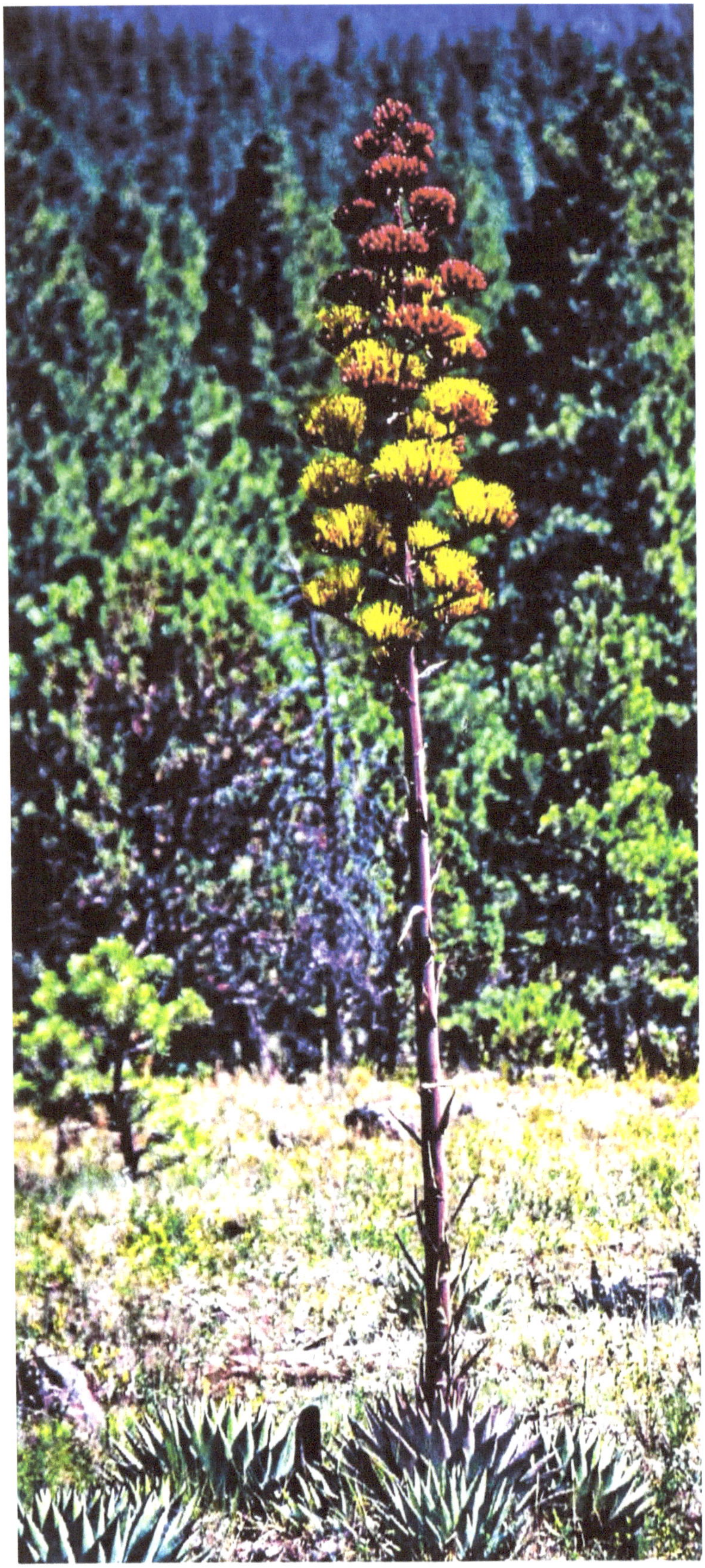

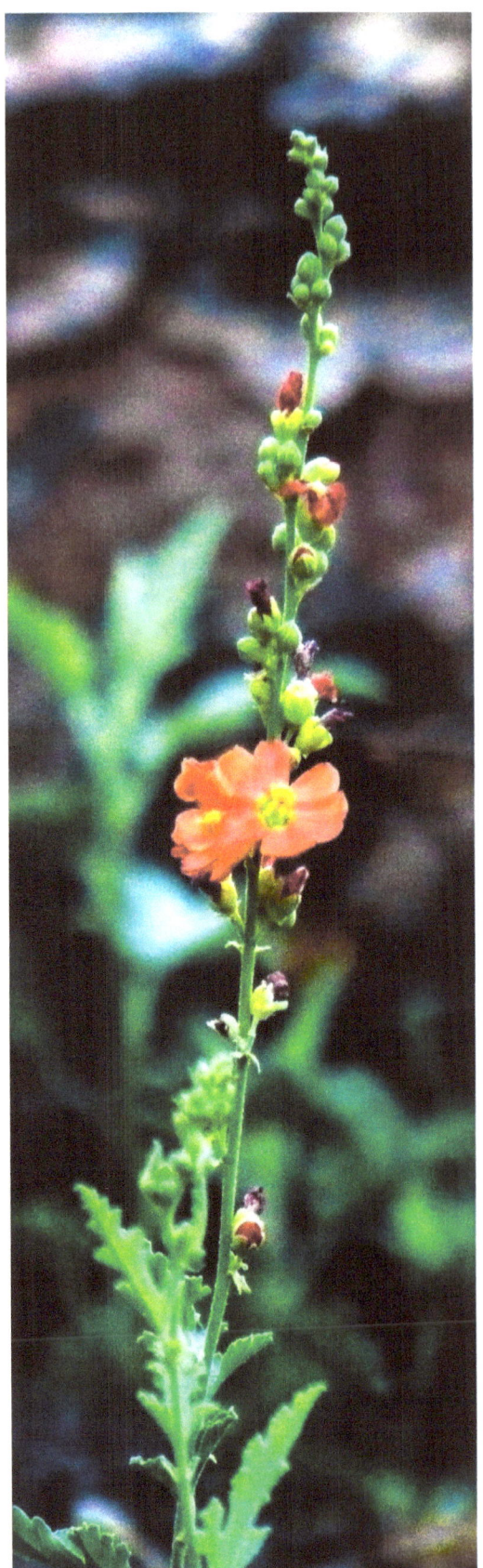

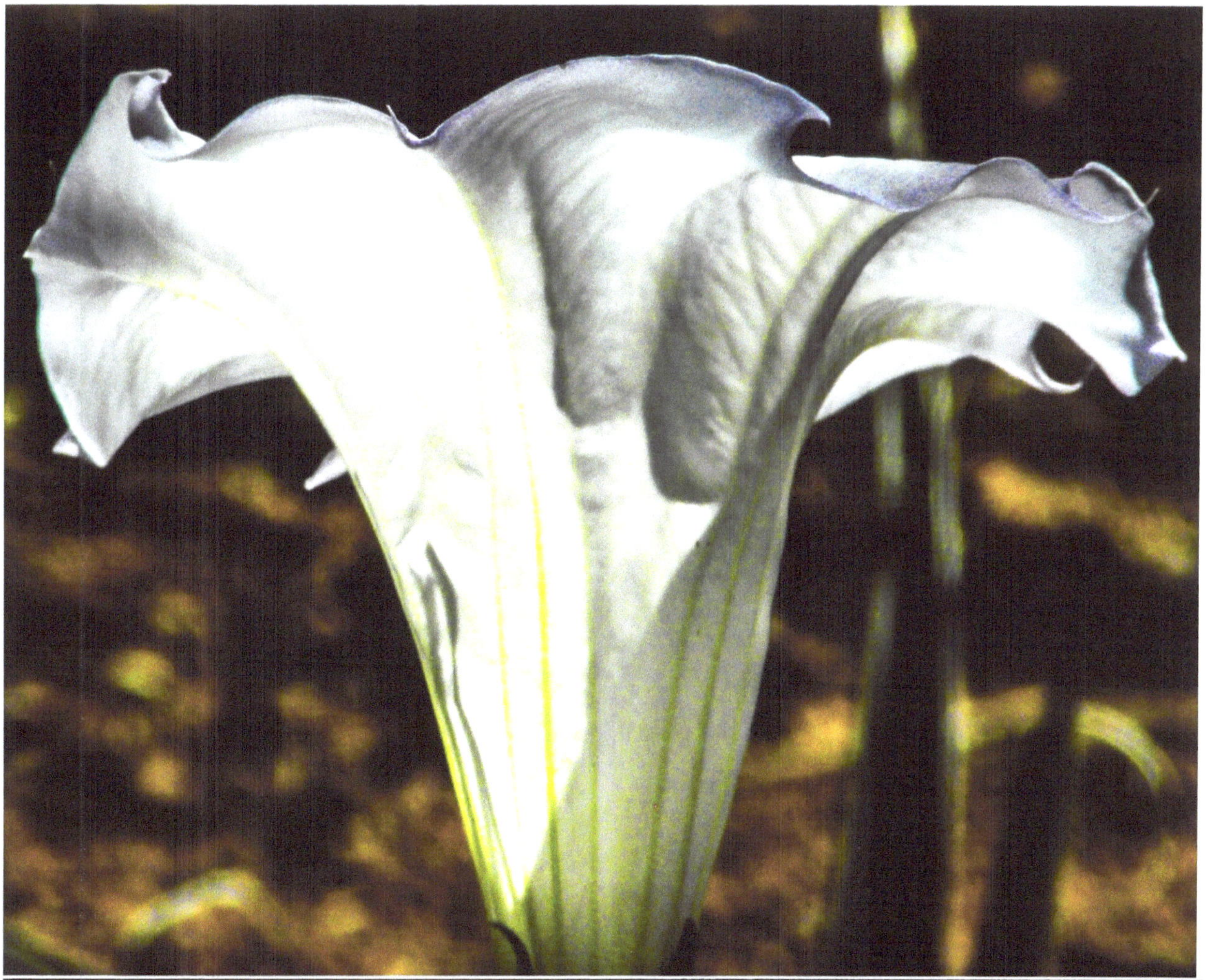

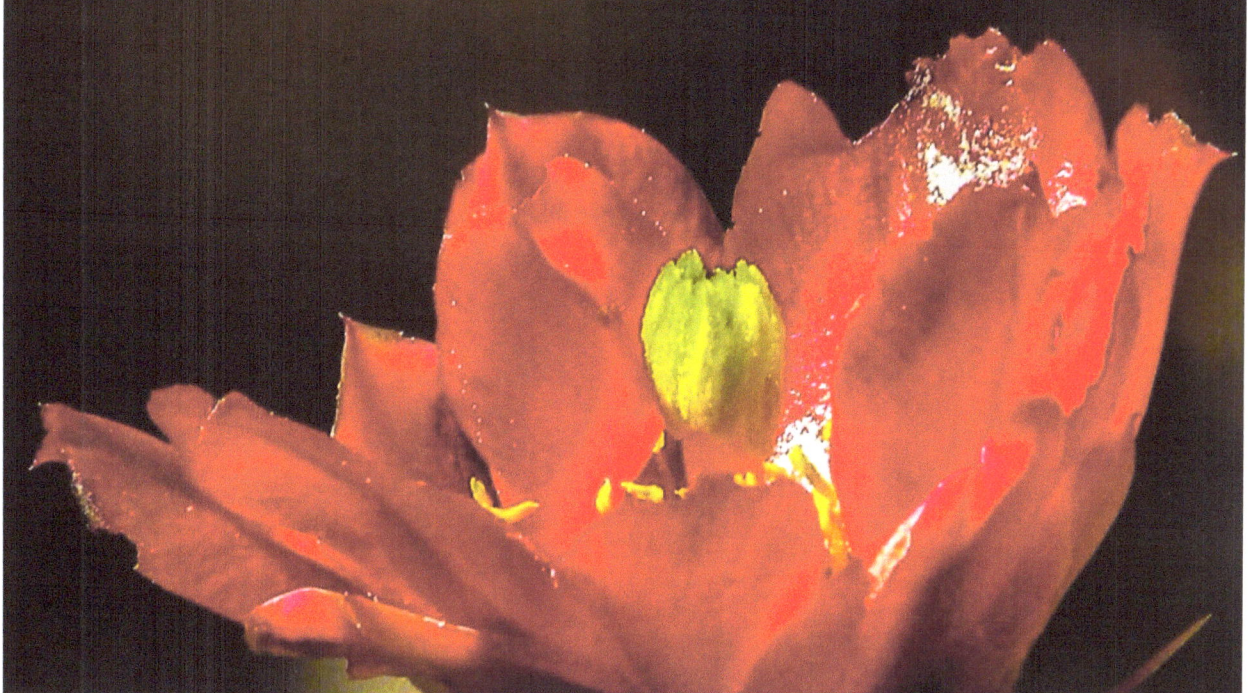

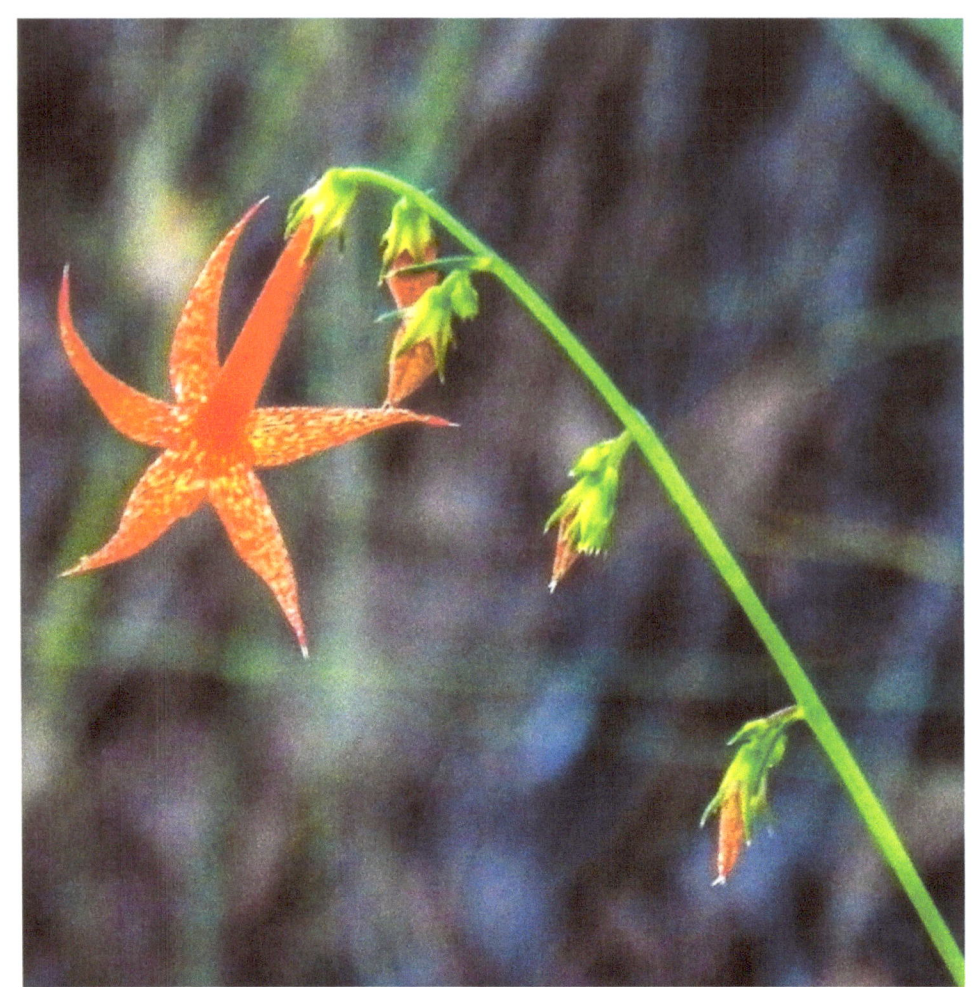

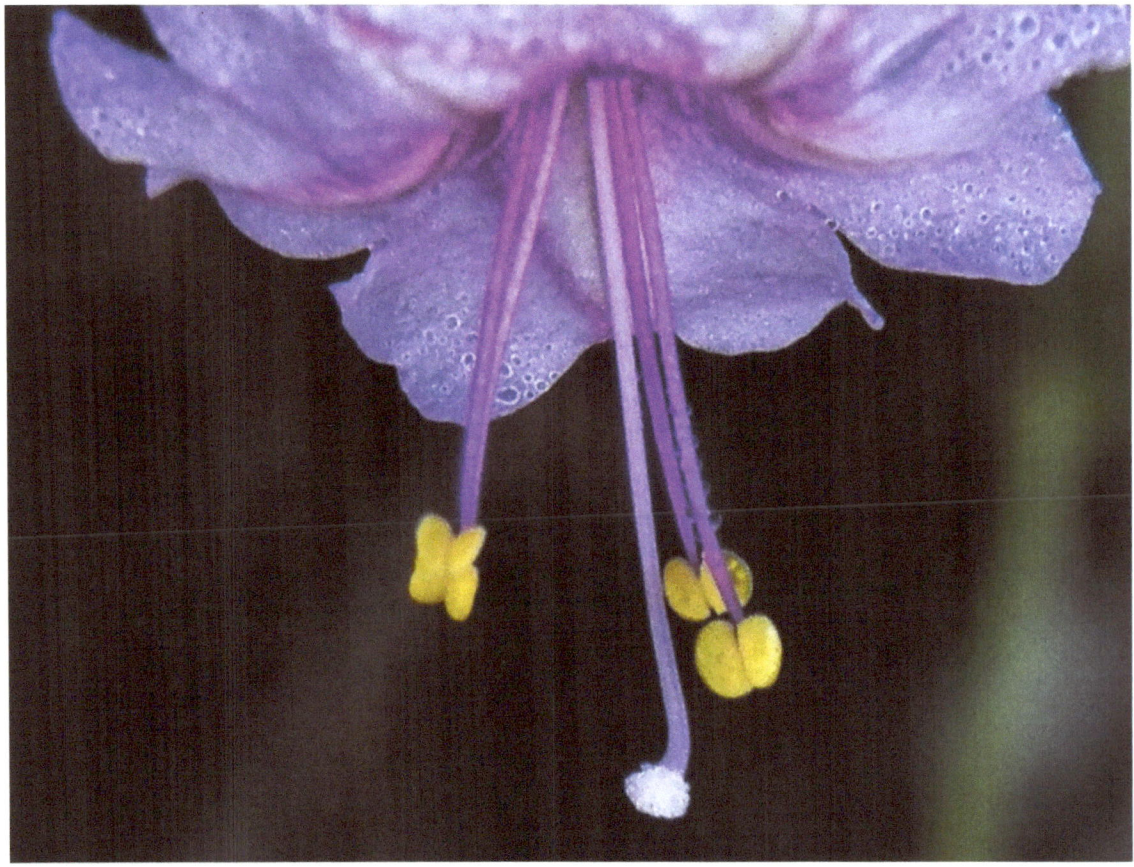